WALKING

on

WATER

TIM SEEBER

WESTBOW
PRESS®
A DIVISION OF THOMAS NELSON
& ZONDERVAN

WestBow Press books may be ordered through booksellers or by contacting:

WestBow Press
A Division of Thomas Nelson & Zondervan
1663 Liberty Drive
Bloomington, IN 47403
www.westbowpress.com
844-714-3454

ISBN: 979-8-3850-1352-4 (sc)
ISBN: 979-8-3850-1353-1 (hc)
ISBN: 979-8-3850-1351-7 (e)

Library of Congress Control Number: 2023922842

Print information available on the last page.

WestBow Press rev. date: 12/08/2023

Dedicated to my parents, Bill and Eunice, whose
faith and love helped me learn how to get out of my
boat and not worry about my feet getting wet

CONTENTS

INTRODUCTION

ONE OF THE MORE FAMILIAR Gospel accounts took place on the Sea of Galilee. Jesus' disciples were on a boat ride that included quite a surprise. In the darkest part of the night, they saw a shape moving toward them across the water. Terror struck their hearts as they feared it was a ghost. Fear turned to relief as they realized it was Jesus, walking on water.

Because the story is so familiar, we often fail to consider how terrifying this moment has to have been. But it was Peter (wasn't Peter always the impulsive one?) who demanded Jesus teach him how to do the same thing. Only Peter thought to ask! Jesus' reply was that if Peter wanted to walk on water he first had to get out of the boat.

Of course, he did, but the impossibility of what he was doing overwhelmed his faith, and slowly Peter started to sink. Jesus grabbed him and returned him to the boat. How silly of Peter. People cannot walk on water, can they?

We have always viewed this story in terms of faith, concluding that if Peter had more faith, he could have done it. But realize how much faith he evidenced by trying! We easily focus on Peter's failure but downplay the faith it took to get out of the boat. Jesus walked on water and invited Peter to do the same.

We often discover the importance in facing the improbable is to first turn things over, look at them inside out, and relearn what we thought we knew. We need to allow faith to lead us out of our familiar boats if we are to grow into the fullness of God's give of faith. And what is faith other than walking on water?

This book is a collection of stories and illustrations from normal, unplanned moments of life. They became my opportunities to get out of the boat and see where Jesus was calling me to walk, swim, or sink into his gift of faith. For me, getting out of the boat is Jesus' call to discipleship, allowing faith to be stronger than confusion, inattentiveness, or fear.

Maybe we can't walk on water, but if we don't get out of the boat, we'll never know, will we? What we always learn from such moments is Jesus daily calls us in many ways to come to Him, to follow Him, to learn from Him. He often does it in surprising ways that are only realized when we are willing to get out of a comfortable and secure boat.

My goal is for these stories to assist in your response to similar daily moments where Jesus is inviting you to join Him in the waters of life.

SLINKYS AND SQUIRRELS

DURING THE COVID-19 PANDEMIC, EVERYONE had different ways of dealing with how to stay home more than they were used to. Some read books that had been untouched for years or started and never finished. Others took to more serious gardening, filling photo albums, or finally beginning to clean out the basement. For some it meant more FaceTime or phone calls with loved ones or taking daily walks again. The walks were appreciated more by the many dogs who had never had so much exercise, but that is another story. And some husbands and wives relearned how to talk with each other in ways they had not done for years. Everyone agreed that how they spent time at home changed drastically due to COVID-19.

For some reason, our backyard became my distraction. To be more precise, I focused on the wildlife that shared the lawn, gardens, and trees in the back of our home. Normally I was so busy that bird feeders were empty for days before I noticed. During that spring when things were still shut down and even our church office was closed for a few weeks, I spent a lot of time sitting in the backyard, reading. And I noticed for the first time why feeders were emptied so quickly. It was the squirrels.

I might have known this at one time but had become too busy over the years to notice, but they were more active and fed more often than I ever realized. There also was much more daily activity by birds and rabbits than I ever had seen. For the first time in many years, I started paying more attention to what I had been too busy to notice. And the squirrels were difficult not to notice.

Our family always laughed at our mom's classic skirmishes with

1

squirrels on her bird feeders, but now I understood her frustration. We had fox squirrels, black squirrels, gray squirrels, and red squirrels. As I began to notice, it seemed as if a single squirrel could empty a feeder in less than an hour. And when they were done, birds and rabbits would hang out in the grass underneath and gorge themselves on the seed, which was dropped as the squirrels attacked the feeders.

One week I had enough of watching squirrels squeeze out the birds and spending more on seed than I wanted to. My plan was to have bird feeders, not squirrel feeders! Somewhere I had heard about hanging a Slinky on the feeder poles to slow the squirrels down. (You do remember those coils of wire we played with as kids?) Of course, I researched this online. Some said the Slinky did the trick, while others said it didn't. My brother told me his squirrel (how can anyone only have one squirrel?) figured the Slinky out in about an hour. But how else was I going to spend my time?

I found two Slinkys at a local store and put them on the pole that hosted the feeders. I filled the feeders, sat on the other side of the yard, and watched. For a couple of hours, the squirrels were afraid of the new look and didn't even try. Then one did, and the others followed. They were quick problem solvers and figured out the Slinkys would stretch to the ground if they hung on them, and then the squirrels used them as ladders and got up to the feeders more easily than before the Slinkys were installed. It was embarrassing to realize how I had wasted so much time and energy on such a useless endeavor rather than something more constructive and rewarding.

We often spend so much time doing certain activities that might be helpful, or maybe aren't, without realizing how easily they can take over our lives, and we are oblivious to everything else going around us. With COVID-19 restrictions, we were forced to use time in new ways. In that period of adjustment, we all realized we had previous preoccupations that we didn't really miss. There were new habits and endeavors that became new patterns of behaviors. As I look back, I have only one question: Why in the world did I let those squirrels take up so much of my time?

This is a reminder of how easily time can get filled and emptied. Even the best of intentions can gradually turn into new patterns or preoccupations that block everything else out of our awareness. It happens all the time in every part of our lives! Distractions can become obsessions, and valuable time can be wasted with things that really don't make that much of a difference in the long run. It is always that way, but this is a momentary example that reminds me of how easily that can happen.

All that frustration and time spent on the squirrels had no effect on them but certainly had on me. I had dealt with what I learned by simply realizing the squirrels needed to eat as much as birds did, and rather than obsess about an inevitable loss, I simply filled feeders when I noticed they were empty and didn't worry as much about whether the squirrels were getting more than their fair share.

Something as simple as squirrels and feeders has become a lesson on how I use my time—or maybe I should say God's time. And it has helped me reflect on what I worry about and what isn't worth fussing about. Rather than a failed experiment and wasted time, it has helped me be more careful about how I do spend time, which in itself is a gift. And at the same time, I have realized I need to quit worrying so much about what I cannot change.

SOMETIMES IT'S A DOG'S LIFE

WHAT IS IT LIKE WHEN your daily routine doesn't change and you feel trapped or are simply bored? How can you work yourself out of grief or depression when you just can't seem to shake free from what is bothering you? There are so many phases in our lives we know are not healthy for us to live in for very long. There are times like these in which we know it is toxic to remain.

Seven years ago, our dog tore her ACL and could only walk on three legs. Surgery was the only solution. It was a success, but we struggled with her postsurgery complications, and our world was turned upside down. Life was not going well for any of us. The surgical repair was a success, but now we had a medium-sized dog that couldn't be allowed on steps, to run, and to jump. We had to keep her confined to the laundry room at night and blocked off the stairs during the day. We couldn't wait for the normal to return. Our home was filled with tension, frustration, and the inability to do what we were normally used to doing.

She could only go outside to take care of her business, and she had to be on a short leash. I had to carry her up and down the deck stairs into the yard. But our waiting got even longer when my wife injured her Achilles tendon. She was in a cast and on crutches and couldn't put any weight on her injured leg. Our downstairs had turned into a hospital ward. It was January. We got fourteen inches of snow, and the temperature dropped to near zero for the next week. And the dog's normal, necessary postdigestive bodily functions ceased. So much for a speedy return to normalcy.

I called the dog's surgeon, and here was how the conversation went:

"Take the dog's temperature." I asked how. He said, "Rectally." I asked him to repeat himself! He said the same thing!

I thought, *Easy for you to say.* So I did the only thing that seemed reasonable. I called my vet and asked if they would be willing to take our dog's temperature. And they did!

Driving there, I remembered to pray—even for the dog! (By the way, if this canine-temperature thing ever comes up for you, it is definitely a two-person job!) And this became a time of reflection as I thought of all the people I had visited over the past week—after surgery, in hospice, coping with chronic illness, struggling with terrible situations at home, and everyone else along the way. It caused me to remember the joy and peace that I encountered in their faith-filled lives.

Our dog eventually wound up with a new lease on life. My wife, Roxanne, and I had more time to be together between her injury and the dog's. And gradually I focused more on what was good rather than what was depressing and inconvenient for me. Best of all, after we left the vet, taking the temperature apparently made our dog Coconut resume her normal bodily functions. Our life hadn't completely been restored to what I wanted, but it was good!

There is nothing more peaceful than being outside at night in the quiet of newly fallen snow—unless you are carrying a dog that cannot do its business. But I learned many things during that time of inconvenience.

I am always amazed at how I worry so much about stuff I can't control and forget to marvel at the miracles God daily and lovingly sends my way. Sometimes life is complicated. Sometimes we are inconvenienced. Sometimes we can't see the end of a situation that is depressing. But if we pay attention, God always finds ways to remind us that we are not alone. In the end, the really big stuff is already covered. When we remember such a love, it can halt our temptation to be worried or depressed.

COME, LORD JESUS,
BE OUR GUEST

WHEN I WAS YOUNGER, I often took my parents for granted. Now that they live in heaven, I would do anything to see them again. But when I remember the relaxed, normal, everyday way that they have made faith in Jesus part of our lives, I can feel their presence still. And one of the neatest things they did was to pray before every meal.

I am now so used to saying "come, Lord Jesus," before every meal that I often just do it without knowing why. Dad and Mom taught it by example, doing it day after day, meal after meal. "Come, Lord Jesus, be our guest and let these gifts to us be blessed. Amen." Those are very simple words, so easy to remember, but it is incredible how much can be said in this special prayer.

Of course, Jesus is always with us, but when we take time away from hunger or a rushed schedule and invite Jesus to join us at the table, we can't help but understand what a powerful moment of faith that is. Would we leave Jesus standing at the door if he knocked? Would we ignore him if he sat next to us in the park? As we are blessing the food, it is such a powerful act of love to remember to invite Jesus to sit down with us. It isn't that he needs an invite, but think about why it is important.

Remember your days in the school cafeteria when everyone got to their tables before you and it looked as if you might be alone? Or ignored? Remember how good if felt when someone invited you to sit with them? How good that felt? One of the gifts of Jesus's journey into our world is to help us understand how to be loved and how to love. His presence is an invitation to know God is close at hand.

"Come, Lord Jesus," is a loving invitation, but it also serves as a reminder he is already and always standing nearby. As we speak such a prayer, it is like inviting a loved one or friend to take a seat and join us. Whenever someone brings us a gift, the next step is to open it. And in unwrapping a gift, we become connected with the giver. This prayer reminds us that in our meal we open gifts of food, nourishment, and family togetherness. And we begin by welcoming the Giver of all gifts.

Certainly, we want God to bless such a moment, to make it a special time, a holy time. We want God to do for us what the gift is intended to do. And in such a time of faithful response, the flavor and feel of the meal is truly changed.

At the Last Supper, Jesus did the same thing as he blessed the bread and wine, and they were changed into more than just food. And in that meal of the new community, we are fed the same gift as the disciples. "Let these gifts to us be blessed" is more than a request for Jesus to act. It is also a statement of faith that reminds us that when Jesus touches anything, it has a new purpose and has the potential of being something more.

What a reminder that gifts of God are meant for more than what might be apparent at first glance. What God blesses becomes a miracle in many ways, and how neat it is for us to handle and share what God has blessed.

Isn't it amazing how a simple prayer can say and do so much? At home, we say it out loud. Sometimes in a restaurant we say it out loud as well and other times silently. But it is part of our routine. It keeps us from taking Jesus or his gifts in our lives for granted—ever!

"Come, Lord Jesus, be our guest and let these gifts to us be blessed. Amen." In such a simple prayer, a meal becomes a time of worship. As we leave the table, our worship continues as we share the gifts of our lives, which are always blessed by the touch of God.

Never forget: with God there is always more than meets the eye. In such a simple prayer, we learn and remember some of the most important issues of faith, living, and loving and are reminded of whose we are! My parents and this prayer have taught me that there is much that I should never take for granted.

CHANGE HAS ALWAYS
BEEN THE NEW NORMAL

CHANGE IS CHANGE, AND A pattern that lasts for any number of weeks or months becomes normal. And when anything changes, it has changed and will never be the same again. Rather than waiting on pins and needles for a dramatic revelation or breakthrough, just consider how often we learn to cope or deal or readjust. This is simply part of living the reality of each new day.

Let me use the example of our pet dogs. For sixteen years, we had a rescue dog named Coconut that we got as a puppy. She had beautiful white fur, was full of energy, and was a great pet. Every time we took her for a walk, people remarked they had never seen a dog like her. She was easy to love and fit right in. She was the queen of the house.

Along the way we got another dog from SPCA, named Winston. He was a four-year-old beagle with a notched ear and crooked teeth and terrified of any noise. He was likely abused as a puppy, was the runt of the litter, and had many barriers to overcome. To top it off, he wasn't the brightest bulb on the planet, but who cannot love a beagle? But Coconut was the queen and definitely ruled the roost.

When Coconut died, we were devastated. We only had Winston for about five years, and even though we tried to treat both of them the same, he was low man on the totem pole. When Coconut died, we wondered how Winston would do with no companion and how we would do with no Coco.

Over the next few months, I noticed something I hadn't planned on. Winston was getting attention and love that was never a part of his early years. Gradually he became more animated and actually showed some personality (if that is a proper term for a dog), but coming out from Coconut's shadow, he came into his own. Change had brought change; what was normal now was different from the past.

Change can either paralyze people or empower them. It can make us fearful of tomorrow or bring new passion and excitement we have not known before. What is in the past is in the past. What is normal is what we experience now. My grandparents grew up with radio but no television. Their cars had no air-conditioning or power steering. Their iceboxes were cooled with blocks of ice. Mom's uncles farmed in Arkansas until the 1990s and never did have electricity. Airplanes gave way to jets. Rotary phones and party lines were replaced with cell phones. You know the deal. Change can be difficult, but it is part of life. Either we deal with what becomes normal or we get left in the dust.

Jesus had the same problem with his disciples. They were so excited to be part of a new movement with such a wonderful teacher. They couldn't believe the miracles and the parables. They loved the crowds and felt so proud to be part of the inner circle. Their old normal was different from their new one. They were ready to have name tags with their job titles and for new offices and reputations that went along with being part of Jesus's band of disciples.

And then Jesus told them about what would come next. He would suffer and die and rise again. Then they would become the leaders who would do for others what he had done for them. That would be their new normal. But they panicked as that was not what they had signed up for. They were no different in that moment from what we are today as we wander through changing cultural norms, contentious elections, and wars across the globe.

Don't you often wish things remained the way you like them and could live with what is most comfortable? Who needs another computer operating system or enjoys having to program another thermostat or display screen in a car? Why is music so different from when we were young?

We are worried about every new normal, and yet what is so different now from what has ever been? The writer of the book of Hebrews says that Jesus is the same yesterday, today, and tomorrow. That will never change!

His promise to be with us is assured, and his power is part of our life. What, then, is so terrifying about earthly changes when real issues of life and death have been taken care of already?

Change is not as important as what we do in the time of change and with the changes that come. What should always be normal for us is faith, hope, and love, and if these three abide in us, they will be the tools with which we live normally despite the changes around us. The important new normal is what has come with Christmas and Easter. Thus, no matter what we face or what we are called to do, we have already been given the gifts for normal living!

EVERYONE HAS A NAME

NAMING OUR CHILDREN BEFORE THEY were born was difficult, and I was not very helpful in that process. I thought, *How could I name someone before I see who they are?* Yet there needed to be a name ready at birth, and not just any name would do. Choosing names was difficult for me, and yet my children were named perfectly. I am not sure how that happened, but I assumed it was their mother who had a better sense than I had of the new life at hand.

We name things to differentiate them from other things but also as a way of having some control over them. For instance, if I need salt for seasoning, I need to know its name. If I just say, "I need the white stuff," I may get sugar, baking powder, or chalk, and a recipe will be ruined. If I have lost someone I care about in a crowd or because they live far away, I had better know their name, or I may not ever connect again. There is a reason for names.

Our daughter Abby always amazed me with her ability to name her stuffed animals. We went through a phase where she was fascinated by little stuffed animals called Webkinz. They were a marketing success. We had Webkinz everywhere—dogs, cats, bunnies, just to name a few. And along with other stuffed animals of every size, our little girl's room was literally stuffed with animals.

What amazed me was that each and every stuffed animal had a unique name, and Abby never forgot any of them. My favorite game was to line up random Webkinz to see if I would find an animal whose name she had forgotten. And I never did. Amazingly, not only did she come up with names for all but each was remembered as well. Once she named something, she never forgot that name.

That reminds me of a passage that begins the book of Jeremiah where God told him that before he was out of the womb, God knew him! That is amazing! Before Jeremiah was a twinkle in his parents' eyes, he was already embraced by God's love. Jeremiah later said that even before his birth, God knew his name.

Some things make my head hurt as I try to understand them, but what a powerful gift it is to know that God knows us before and after this earthly life. We are part of his eternity, and even though it is more than what we can comprehend, this adds so much peace to my living as we know how special we are to God.

The awareness of having a name that is known by God helps me understand God as one who can pick me out of any crowd, can bring me to his place of nourishment and love, and knows how to reach me when I am lost, afraid, or alone. What's in a name? Think about this: Genesis 1 is all about naming what is important—trees, rivers, streams, planets, moon, star, rain. And now we know that God has a name for each of us as well!

What's in a name? Well, think of it this way: wouldn't it be sad if you were just a nameless, lost soul drifting unconnected without a purpose? On the other hand, anything of value, anything of life, anything touched by God has a name, and God knows that name! So begin each day celebrating that you have been named by God, and he will never forget your name or cease calling to keep you close, nourished, guided, and loved!

For many generations, it was the practice at baptism to give a child a Christian name. (If you ever wondered where the word *christening* came from, now you know!) This was important as baptism is truly a naming ceremony. It is our sacred moment to celebrate the gift of life as coming from God, affirming the purpose and plan God has in loving each of us. It is a reminder that God knows our name, calls us by that name, and promises to walk with us forever.

That is why my grandmother had four names. She was named Katherine Charlotte Thaden at birth, and the name Johanna was added at her baptism. Her parents gave her the birth certificate name, and at baptism her Christian name was added as an act of faith. I really like that idea and wish that we had continued it with our children.

More importantly, it is great that God knows our name. We are important, we are loved, and we will have a forever place next to God.

No matter what you face or fear, God knows your name. He will never forget you! No matter what today or tomorrow brings, God has your name in mind as he reaches out to walk with you like a parent holding a little child's hand. And no matter what you think about your name, God only feels love when he uses it and whispers it into your ear. There is so much in a name, and God will never forget yours!

OLD DOGS, NEW TRICKS

WE HAVE ALL HEARD THAT you can't teach an old dog new tricks. One of the oldest idioms in the English language, it assumes you train a dog either early or never at all. Unfortunately, with our present dog, we have found how true it really is! However, I recently read a study proving old dogs can indeed learn new things. It just takes them longer. So maybe it is a seemingly innocent truism that should be reconsidered.

I guess it makes sense. Habits are harder to change the longer they are practiced. But the dark side of this idiom is that it often isn't used about dogs at all but is a disguised way to talk about people. So we'll think about it in that context.

In some cases, people use this as a cop-out, an excuse not to try or learn anything new. It is easy to resist change, blaming age or being set in one's ways. Too often, we simply don't want to move out of our comfort zone as habits become familiar and easy.

A more disturbing use of this proverb is when a younger person assumes that after age forty, learning ceases, so why even bother with dinosaurs as they can't or won't try to learn anything new? Let me speak to that with a story about Wilma Wertz, a retired eighty-year-old librarian who became a mentor in my first congregation in Toledo.

One day she stopped by after the weekly presentation at the local senior citizen center. Wilma was fit to be tied! A young social worker had just explained to the crowd of energetic and active seniors what it is like to get old. Wilma told me several days later, "If I have one more younger person explain to me what it is like to be old, what will happen next isn't going to be pretty!"

And there you have it! What a great lesson for a young pastor, which was probably why she shared this in the first place. A young social worker was already paralyzed by her stereotype and needed to learn a new trick, which was not to assume age takes away the willingness to learn something new or do something old in a new way.

During the COVID-19 pandemic, we wrestled with new situations we could never have imagined. It became apparent to our congregation that to survive, we needed to learn new tricks, or we would lose our ability to share the wonderful energy and gift of the Gospel of Jesus. This transition was no different from what it was for many of our ancestors who discovered they had to give up the language of their homeland if they were to prosper and succeed in a new land.

Wasn't Jesus's entire ministry about teaching old dogs new tricks? Satan had to learn that death was no longer in his power. The religious leaders had to learn that love for God and neighbor was more important than rituals and rules and regulations. Everyday people needed to learn that God wasn't distant and that they were created to reveal him to the world by how they lived and loved. New tricks for old dogs.

Martin Luther and other reformers realized that the many familiar bells and whistles of the established church needed to be seen not as answers but vehicles to assist in changing hearts hardened by sin into hearts free to be changed by God's love. His efforts were all about new tricks for an old dog. And it worked!

During the effort to maintain contact in a pandemic, when most were isolated and separated by masks and fear, we learned to either learn new tricks or lose the gifts that are so important to our lives of faith. I was not anxious to have to learn how to lead a Zoom meeting or put all the energy into weekly online worship, but without this old dog learning new tricks, I would be paralyzed in the past and unable to carry out my call to serve.

People of all ages slip into habits of selfish behavior and unwillingness to change. Our tendency is to fail to forgive or love when the going gets tough. We find our habits and routines more important than realizing how they may keep us from growing or others from sharing with us.

Parents and children can be even more resistant to change than seniors (who understand all too well how change is what life is all about). In this time of fear about contracting a virus, many have gotten so used to staying masked and distant from others that it might become difficult down the road to relearn how to share and serve face-to-face.

Consider how, over the centuries, the old dog we call the church has had to learn new tricks, moving from Latin to new languages and adopting new cultural realities. For instance, it had to accommodate radio, television, and then the internet. The Gospel never changes, but old dogs keep needing to learn new tricks. And each day is an opportunity for us to learn and celebrate the new tricks that bring us closer to God or loving those around us. That is what the power of the Holy Spirit is for—change!

And if you and I can learn to trust God, to forgive and serve those around us, and to be selfless rather than selfish, I think we can learn how to keep growing in faith and sharing that faith, even if we have to do it in new ways. Habits die hard, but even old dogs can learn new tricks!

SKUNKS

OUR KIDS CAMPED OFTEN WITH good friends of the same age, which made the trips much more enjoyable. One year was especially memorable for reasons we had not anticipated.

One night when the kids were asleep in the tents, we parents were finally rewarded with peace. We sat around the campfire, just enjoying the quiet. My friend Greg and I took a short walk to give our wives a chance to talk about us in private.

We wandered around the campground, just having a guy chat, wondering how many other campers were in the site, and enjoying the stillness, which was the purpose of our getting away. When we got back to the campfire, our wives were still sitting where we left them, but one very quietly, almost in a whisper, said, "Be careful. There are skunks with us, and we don't want you to scare them!" It made sense to us!

We looked, and there were four or five skunks wandering several feet from the mothers of our children. Two were actually stationed under each of the lawn chairs they were sitting on. It appeared to be one of those moments that might disintegrate quickly into a real problem.

We stopped and were motionless. The skunks were scrounging pieces of marshmallows and graham crackers that had fallen by the fire. We kept very quiet, just waiting to see if we were going to run or not, as there was nothing we could do to change the standoff we were observing.

After about ten minutes, the food was gone, and the skunks wandered away, with their distinctive black and white tails following them into the woods. No damage was done, and there were no lingering reminders in the air of their visit. It was all good. Or so I thought, until about two in the morning.

I woke up and needed to head to the outhouse, but as I was about to open the door of our tent, I heard a rustling just outside. We didn't have a screen on that side of the tent, so I couldn't see what was there but assumed it had to be the skunks, back for more food. I was trapped! And I was afraid.

There was nothing I could do but wait them out, and for the next four hours, every time I thought it was safe to leave the tent and take care of business, I heard that same rustling sound that could only mean a skunk was lying in wait to ambush me. It was the most uncomfortable night of camping I could remember as I couldn't go back to sleep, and I couldn't get out to do what I needed to do.

It seems silly now to think about how I allowed a noise to trap me in a tent without even knowing for certain what that noise was. But the thought of a skunk attack kept me paralyzed in fear. I know it sounds ridiculous, but who wants to deal with a skunk in the woods? Obviously, I survived. I don't even know for sure if there was a skunk! Maybe I was dreaming, and maybe I was just so convinced that the skunk had returned that my imagination got the better of me.

In a strange way this felt familiar, like similar struggles during our early encounter with a pandemic. We worried about where we could go and what we could do. We worried about how to avoid getting sick and how long that current darkness would remain. We couldn't relax, and worry was everywhere. That was all made complicated by the incessant drama and fears of political and social upheaval. We worried about being misunderstood. We worried about the future. We wondered if and when we might finally find calm and peace without all the fears that surrounded us.

How often does fear, whether rational or not, paralyze us and keep us trapped behind closed doors or make us afraid of what is lurking around the next corner? Even Jesus's disciples had trouble leaving the safety of an upper room, overwhelmed by the fear of what might or could happen. Throughout their classroom lessons with Jesus, over and over again, he had to dispel their fears and help them learn that faith is about letting go of what can't be controlled and trusting that God will be there no matter what does or doesn't happen next.

There was a day when Jesus asked if worry could cause anyone to add a single hour to their life. Over and over, he encouraged his flock not to worry or be afraid. In such a simple way he shared a powerful love. The same voice that created a universe and made a storm on a lake stand still reassures us with those simple words: "Fear not, little flock." What peace from knowing there is a shepherd on duty and neither skunk nor COVID-19 nor the wrong candidate getting elected can separate us from God's love or his care and protection!

In hindsight, even the worst attack from a skunk wouldn't have changed my life, and yet I allowed fear to take hold when there were other more positive options available. And I am certain we will find the same truth in even the more difficult and traumatic moments of life. Fear not, little flock. Fear not!

FORGIVE?

WE HAD SOME MINOR VANDALISM on our church as someone with a can of spray paint and no creative outlet decided to decorate our front doors with angry words and provocative images. We have all witnessed similar graffiti in other places and don't give it a second thought unless we are directly affected or have to endure the effort of cleaning up someone else's mess. There are so many bored, angry, and unstable people who find ways such as this to satisfy inner frustrations or attempt to get attention. Children just throw things across the room or have temper tantrums. As we get older, we don't always mature but simply find bigger and louder platforms for similar venting.

Now paint is easy to clean up. There are more intense actions that bring greater emotional or physical harm, such as the abuse of children or spouses, civil disobedience, destroying a reputation, prejudice, harassment, murder, and war. Understanding the motivation for such outbursts never excuses them. All we can do is be overwhelmed as we realize how much anger, frustration, and passion for revenge filter through so much of the world in which we live.

We often find ourselves responding to similar outbursts in a world where so many feel their own needs and feelings are more important than love for God or neighbor. No one is immune, and anyone who assumes differently needs only to look in a mirror and face times and ways in which selfish reaction has overpowered any sense of proportion or servant love.

There is so much that is beyond our understanding and control. Often, our attempts to play God and dispense justice only deal with symptoms rather than the disease that poisons thoughts and actions. Here is what I do know: From the cross, Jesus prayed that God forgive those who sought his death, saying they didn't understand what they were doing. Such a loving request is beyond human understanding. He didn't condone the action but prayed that God would change lives through his forgiving love. There is no guarantee that will work, but it is God's goal. And it introduces us to our mission as those who are gifted with faith.

Jesus cautioned against condemning a splinter in someone else's eye while failing to see beyond the log that clouds our own perspective. He meant that we don't always filter reality as well as we think and often are blinded by our own imperfections. Such guidance reminds me to be cautious in how I judge the thoughts, words, and deeds of someone else.

When in doubt, begin with love. There are no guarantees, as Jesus's crucifixion has proved, but I do believe that is where we are called to begin. On the cross he said, "Father, forgive them."

After the vandalism at church, we still had to clean graffiti off our doors and file police reports, but it was then more important to move on and not dwell on the weakness or brokenness of someone else. I should have, but probably hadn't, taken a moment to pray that God would find a way to break into that life, which was so disturbed. A good rule of thumb for each of us is to first look in the mirror to see where we have fallen short before we begin to attack someone else.

God loves the whole world, despite all that is wrong with it. If God can love so much, maybe I need to learn to attempt a similar response. God has never said it will be easy, but we do know that is where we may begin. Words are cheap. The cross is expensive. Maybe we shouldn't let that gift go to waste!

TAKING SIDES

IN MY FIRST CONGREGATION, I watched in pain a couple who decided to divorce. They had been loved by everyone in the congregation and were extremely active in many ministries. As painful as the divorce was for their family, I am not sure they were prepared for losing their friends as well. I was close to each of them, but after the divorce, I never saw either of them again—it was not my choice but theirs.

Several friends told me they couldn't associate with either husband or wife for fear of offending the other. The pain all felt for what was lost was intensified as none of us were used to seeing either alone, especially not with someone new. Over time, others took a similar stance rather than get dragged into the conflict. And this couple, who was no longer a couple, simply disappeared.

In a sense, being a citizen of a country, an employee in a company, or a member of a congregation is like being in a marriage. We are in a relationship that we have responsibility to maintain and keep healthy, but often, brokenness creeps in.

In a perfect world, it would be wonderful to see respect, a willingness to listen, and a commitment to common goals to keep us engaged with everyone else for the health of that relationship. That would be such a healthy vision for any couple, member of Congress, neighbor, or people from different cultures as well—to have others willing to embrace, listen, and love rather than take sides when mistrust or differing views begin to divide.

How often do we rush to take sides rather than consider a different direction? When might it be healthier to seek for an avenue to restore rather than destroy a community full of lives that are loved by God? That is an important question for all of us as we live in a world that wants to see everything in black and white and has no room for shades of gray. There are so many choices. Masks or no masks? Restaurants open or closed? Virtual or in-person schools? Hymnals or hymns projected on screens? Democrat or Republican? Impeachment or time to move on?

Our faith lifts the image of a God who stands in the midst of any conflict or dispute to reach out in love for the purpose of healing and restoring what has been lost. The image of a cross with arms reaching out in two directions is a wonderful illustration of God's love in the midst of a conflicted world. From the cross, Jesus reminds us that his love is for all no matter how far apart any may have moved from the other.

If God has gone to such lengths to forgive and love even me, why will I ever be unwilling to begin to understand my relationship with and my call to reach out even to those who have upset me or whom I am nervous being around? Even if there is no guarantee of success, what do I lose if I try?

The most valued mentor in my life has once told me that whoever defines the question wins the argument. I have never forgotten that. If I believe the husband is responsible for the divorce, it may be difficult to defend or support him in any way. If I believe the wife is responsible, the same will be true in a completely different direction. What changes when we begin by admitting the obvious, which is that none of us is perfect?

No political leader or party is perfect. No relationship is perfect. No union or business leader is perfect. No point of view is not already tainted by sin before it is even expressed. No curriculum is without faults. Nobody has a corner on perfect truth.

On the other hand, God's love is so great that he has come into all this nonsense to bring us back to our senses. And he does so by seeking not to destroy what is broken but to restore its potential in forgiveness and love.

That begins with the love Jesus taught being not only my focus but also the light I seek to share. If I am going to choose sides, that is the choice that allows me to offer the most positive and constructive assistance to others. It may not be the easiest path to follow, but there is a reason why that is the path Jesus has chosen for me. If I am going to cross a bridge, the one Jesus built at Bethlehem and Calvary has a more lasting and loving journey to offer. Such a journey may not win a lot of votes, but it will begin to bring light into the darkness that seems to shadow over more than what we want.

MORE THAN A RAINBOW

IN GRADE SCHOOL WE LEARNED about prisms. If we held one up to sunlight, all the colors of the rainbow were projected onto a piece of white paper. It was like magic!

It boggles my mind to imagine all those colors hidden inside sunlight. Rainbows are a result of the same process as when sunlight shines through raindrops, which act as prisms. That is not magic but a miracle. Even the simplest parts of creation cause wonder and awe.

Was the rainbow Noah saw the first ever, or was it simply the first time a rainbow held meaning and promise for Noah? The Bible is full of instances of God's presence giving meaning beyond time and space. Whatever God touches makes miracles out of the mundane.

What have you seen so often that it is taken for granted? And what about those showstopping moments when you have flashes of inspiration in an ordinary moment? How often has beauty filled what you have considered ordinary before? It is amazing what happens as we see how God's fingerprint or voice gives new meaning to every gift of his creation.

In high school we have learned how cells divide and the process by which an embryo grows as cells differentiate into unique roles. Over time, what has begun with something tiny and simple becomes a complex life with multiple organs, functions, and potentials. Science can explain the facts of life, but the true meaning of life cannot be explained without the miracle of God's touch.

When my first child was born, scientific fact was quickly forgotten. I was mesmerized by her umbilical cord, which looked like something out of a science fiction movie. I knew it was the connection and lifeline that had nourished her in her mother's womb, but the only appropriate explanation for what I watched was "miracle." And in my tears, I am certain there were little rainbows clinging to my eyelids and flowing down my cheeks.

My guess is Noah had seen his share of rainbows but thought little of them. They certainly never had the meaning that came after the great Flood and God's promise that was attached. When God promised every rainbow would be a reminder, he was right! From then on, every bow of color in the sky was a miracle of hope as every rainbow contains God's touch and his voice!

So much of life is filled with stuff we have seen before—a sunset, a bird's nest, a shooting star, a waterfall, a nursing infant, leaves changing color, puppies licking someone's cheek. There are textbook explanations, but as we confess God's plan and purpose, the ordinary is seen as miraculous.

Because of God's touch and tone, every moment—from rainbows to thunder, from sunrise to seasons—has a message heard loud and clear. The incredible complexity of God's creative energy is the life of creation.

Photography is a favorite hobby for me. It has forced me to slow down and pay attention. A photo is simply reflected light captured as an image. As I begin to develop negatives, use software to remove a speck of dust from an image, or crop out something that is a distraction, I have learned about patience. It is embarrassing to admit how much time can be spent on a single image, but such a focus has helped me see what is often so easy to miss. Over and over, as I look at a photo, I see details I have never noticed. And then I look closer and find even more.

What is more, this has helped me slow down and pay more attention to life all around me, even when I am not taking pictures. I am learning to see shades of color I have never noticed before. There are patterns and reflections everywhere. I hear sounds in a new way when I take time to listen. Even the voices of those I love change as I hear them as the miracles God has brought into my life. In the quiet of mediation and prayer, I have found the same to be true. In such moments of clarity, the meaning and my relation to the world around me change as well.

In slowing down, I am learning to hear God's voice or see his fingerprints, which are easy to miss when I am in a rush. His creative touch and promise of hope change the shape and tone of all that I encounter.

For instance, when I stare at the shapes and colors of clouds that gradually change as the sun dips under the horizon, I cannot help but see the miracle of what God has created.

I am a work in progress just as we all are, but slowing down and listening or feeling God's presence is part of that process. Noah would never take a rainbow for granted again as God's voice would always be the sound of those beautiful colors in the sky. The same can be true for all of us. We are often so busy, distracted, or anxious to move from one moment to the next that we often forget to see and hear what God has placed right before us.

Daily we must find opportunities to slow down and consider what God is doing in every miraculous moment of creation. As we do so, we are more likely to see his fingerprints more clearly and even begin to hear his voice!

Noah no longer saw just a rainbow but God's voice in color! God's fingerprints are on everything we see. His voice is in everything that is. If we can look at life as Noah learned to look at rainbows, we will learn how to live.

EARTH DAY

GENESIS STARTED WITH THE PROCLAMATION that everything began when God created the heavens and the earth. On that first day, all the earth came into being.

I was in college when the first Earth Day was held. It was a call to pay more attention to creation than had been given since the beginning of the industrial age. As a result, rivers, streams, and the air we breathe are certainly much cleaner now than fifty years ago! Anyone who remembers driving through the smog around Gary's steel mills will agree. Once upon a time, the Cuyahoga River in Cleveland was so polluted that it actually caught on fire. Much has changed, and litter cleanup, bottle deposits, and recycling are now expected rather than hoped for.

In reviewing God's plan in Genesis for the harmony and relationships of his creation, there is much to remember. Sin is the brokenness that has disturbed what God has intended. Whether we speak of murder or pollution, we understand each is a misuse of God's gifts and insensitivity to the love that has made all things be. As Christians, we understand Genesis is a reminder of God's purpose and plan and begins the revelation of all God has done to get us back on track. In the miracle of Jesus's life, death, and resurrection, God has not only remedied our guilt and earthly death but also shared a model of how we are to live with God and neighbor as objects of our respect, love, care, and servanthood. God's plan is about loving relationships. It is about restoring creation.

Practical concern for our care of the earth initiated many of the ecological efforts and issues that continue today. But the first real Earth

Day was when God created this planet. Creation was not a random, unfocused, arbitrary series of events but the orderly plan of a loving God. Too often, we have allowed selfishness and immediate need to be more important than a faithful response to God and stewardship of his gifts. Too often, we act as if the planet were under our control rather than realizing it is a gift from the Creator. And God is still involved in his creative way more than we are willing to give him credit for.

When we keep water clean to celebrate and protect a gift from God, it has more value than simply responding out of fear of what chemicals have been added. Rather than reacting only when self-interests are involved, we should respond to any and all of God's gifts by seeing them for what they really are. God has gifted us with so much, and the proper way to accept a gift is to use if for its intended purpose. That not only allows a gift to be useful but also honors the giver in a selfless way. There is a difference between doing something because the law demands it and doing so out of love for what God has given.

One Christmas my son saved until he could buy me a very special gift. It was a ceiling rack for pots and pans to hang over the kitchen island. My first reaction was to remark that our ceiling was too low for it to be practical. In doing so, I ignored his love and hurt his feelings when my first reaction should have been loving thanks. We could have then talked later about replacing the gift with a rack that would fit. But I had polluted the river of our love and had littered the kitchen with the insensitivity of my reaction. Over the years I have learned many lessons, but this was one of the toughest for me to forget.

It is still embarrassing to remember! It is even more painful to realize how easily and often we have disrespected God's gifts of creation that are all around us. Whether taking them for granted or using them selfishly, we often fail to glorify God and the loving gifts he has created.

Many native peoples who lived in America for centuries before our ancestors showed up were more attuned to that balance than many of the Christians who settled here. When Lakota Sioux, for instance, killed a buffalo, every part of the animal had a use to keep them alive. Nothing was wasted. And they thanked the Creator God for such a gift and felt they were honoring the gift in how it was used. Anyone who has to live off the land understands the miraculous gift it truly is.

We can easily become selfish and forget gifts are gifts. They are not rights. They are never deserved. Otherwise, we will not use the word *gift*. And what God has created, planting us in the middle of it, is certainly a great gift of his! That certainly changes our perspective and what it means to give God glory.

One day Jesus spoke to the people who worried and sought more control over life. He told them the wealth and beauty of Solomon's creations couldn't hold a candle to the beauty of a simple lily of the field.

If we understand how to live with love for God and neighbor, the need for laws fades away. The gift of life on the earth is not for us to control and manipulate but for us to steward as our act of worship and sharing. It is not my water to control but God's gift for the good of his world. It is not my air to breathe but God's life that fills my lungs. Life on the earth is a gift given in love and worthy of the love of the Giver. We are called to a unique approach to living, and the result is our opportunity to be a light to the rest of the world. Think about it. Give thanks. And then live in loving response.

CANARY IN A CAGE

WHEN WE TOOK OUR FIRST hike in the mountains of Colorado, we were amazed at how quickly our breathing became labored, and minor symptoms of altitude sickness emerged. Our homes have carbon monoxide detectors to detect a poison we cannot smell that if inhaled too long can bring sickness and death. For many years British coal miners took canaries into the mines as early warnings of the presence of odorless poisonous gases. When a canary died, the miners knew that they had precious little time to escape the mine. Breathing poisonous air or having a lack of oxygen brings death.

It is interesting that we take for granted some of the most important things in life. For instance, we never think about each breath we take or each beat of our heart; unless there is a problem, then we pay attention. And yet when we learn to pay attention and care for how we breathe, we can sometimes keep ourselves from the troubling effects of weakened lungs or damaged hearts.

When God created the world, his breath spoke the perfection of life into being, and Adam and Eve breathed in and out that perfect paradise. God's Word was all it took for all to be, and it was good. His holy breath was what creation breathed in and was expected to breathe out. God's love was accepted and then was shared!

But the voice of a serpent polluted the air, and each breath after that was filled with the poison of selfishness, envy, and greed. That filled good lungs with a spiritual poison that led to the brokenness and death we referred to as sin. The perfection of creation was destroyed as Satan tainted life with his foul promises and the poison of selfishness, sin, and death.

Life is often like what it must be for coal miners deep in the darkness of a cave. Often, we trust our senses and artificial lights but are unaware of what we are really breathing in and out. We can easily be hurt or damaged by others, often catching us completely by surprise. In the same spirit, we can breathe out selfishness or insensitivity without even being aware of how it affects someone else or the people we care about.

The good news that changed the playing field for all time (like a canary in a coal mine) is what God has done for us in the life, death, and resurrection of Jesus. Jesus came to this earth to breathe our poisoned air for us. He accepted our death and suffered for our sin. He wasn't forced to do this like a caged canary but willingly came as a helpless infant and suffered a sentence and crucifixion he didn't deserve. Unlike a dying canary in a cave, he escaped the tomb and changed our living and our dying forever.

We take so much for granted, but God never fails to appreciate us. With every breath we take and every step we make, he has been there already and is with us now. The term *Holy Spirit* literally means "holy breath" or, for our purpose, the breath of God. His Holy Spirit comes into our lungs to cleanse us from the stale sin of Satan's foul poison so that we may learn to be filled again with forgiving love and to live with servanthood and peace. What we breathe in is what we will breathe out. In this journey, we are given a moment to reconsider how far we can get on our own breath and how far God can carry us on his lifesaving breath and Spirit.

Your life is a gift from God. As we love God and neighbor, we are simply breathing out what has come to us by grace. Seeking to maintain that supply of life is a better path to travel than to inhale the deceptively sweet but deadly breath of that serpent that reared its ugly head in the garden. And the good news is that even when we find ourselves in the cave of death, the breath of God's Holy Spirit will lead us safely home.

When we learn how to breathe the right air, we truly find peace!

EASTER BUNNY

MY MOTHER SPENT HER LAST years on the earth in a care facility in another state. One of my visits to see her happened to be the day after Easter. I arrived in the parking lot and started gathering the goodies I had brought along for Mom. As I got out of my car, I was distracted to see some commotion on the other side of the parking lot.

There were a large Easter bunny and several helpers coming from the administration building and heading to the building where Mom was living. I assumed it was the entertainment for the residents that day.

Still in the Easter worship mode, I did a quick adjustment as I saw someone dressed in a bunny costume, which was not something one normally expected to see. In turn, it caused me to reflect on how we would celebrate holidays that began as holy days. There is nothing wrong with Easter bunnies and baskets just as there is nothing wrong with Santa and gifts under a tree. And I will be the first to admit I miss having my children around for these special celebrations because it is so much fun decorating eggs and filling baskets, just as it is fun watching them open gifts under the tree on Christmas morning. That large-as-life Easter bunny caught me off guard!

When we first experienced the worldwide pandemic of COVID-19, we didn't celebrate Easter as we used to. We were under quarantine, and there was no Easter worship with brass and hymns and everyone celebrating an empty tomb. Our worship service the day before was more special than normal as we were able to gather again in our normal place of worship.

That service was a reminder not to take any of God's gifts for granted as we never know what tomorrow will bring. Easter changes the playing field, and no matter what virus or political crisis or family disturbances emerge, God has set us free to live with him forever, and that allows each day to become a celebration of Easter.

I love Easter bunnies and Santas, but I am even more moved by God's love for me, which was revealed in a manger and given power by an empty tomb. Don't take for granted what grace makes available every day! However we do or don't celebrate at special times of the year, always remember that every day is filled with the joy of Christmas and the miracle of an empty tomb. And that is the best news we have ever been given and is more than enough to change how we live and love, how we hope and dream, how we give thanks and serve.

I was glad for the Easter bunny surprise that Mom and the other residents would share in, but it also helped me remember that God has made every day a holy day, full of his gifts of grace, ready to be opened, celebrated, and shared. Why ever take Easter for granted, no matter how we remember or where we celebrate?

HAULING TRASH

SEVERAL TIMES A YEAR THE city trucks pick up all the junk that is cleaned out of basements, attics, and garages. For weeks neighborhood curbsides are lined with mattresses, old bookshelves, discarded water heaters, broken lawn equipment, and rusted-out grills. And that is just the beginning.

As soon as junk starts piling on the streets, there is the noise every night of pickup trucks trolling the streets, looking for useful junk, such as metal for recycling or old motors that can be repaired. Couches, chairs, and broken tables likely wind up in summer lake cottages. Like ants crawling over food dropped in the grass at a picnic, there are pickup trucks combing our streets night after night, looking for something useful in what others feel is only junk.

There are so many issues at play here that it is difficult to know where to begin. For a few years we didn't put stuff out because we forgot. Then I felt guilty for not contributing to the effort. Unwilling to part with junk that had a few more years of life, I hung on and wouldn't let go, even though I should have. As I finally surrendered useless stuff, I'd never forget my dismay when the scavengers didn't want anything I had thrown out. I was devastated! The city would still haul it, but what was wrong with my discards that no one else found them valuable? Think about how absurd that sounds, and yet my feelings were really hurt!

There are so many lessons in this effort. Primarily it is a reminder of how much useless stuff we cling onto in our lives. We have hidden guilt, embarrassing moments, and decisions we would rather forget, and they are hung on to like junk in a closet. Sooner or later, we need to let go, for until we clean them out, those issues can haunt us and remind us of what we will just as soon forget.

In theological terms we talk about confession as surrendering our brokenness and mistakes to God so that he can carry it away like those junk trucks that haul useless items out of our neighborhood. Confession unburdens the soul, and as we confess to someone who has hurt us, it begins the wonderful renewal of healing and peace.

There is something cathartic about letting go of what can't help us and what is not useful. We should learn to do it more often than we do. And what's most surprising is that we often find out that what we are so embarrassed about or fear no one will even notice are the most important things to surrender. When it is time to let go, it is time to surrender. And once we do, walk away. It doesn't matter at that point how anyone else responds or even notices.

And the biggest lesson comes when the city finally wanders through and makes sure that no scraps, leftovers, and unwanted junk remain. That is so much like the forgiving love of a servant shepherd like Jesus. What we can't deal with, he has. What we can't surrender, he carries on his back. What we are embarrassed about, he accepts anyway, and he offers only the freedom of forgiving love in return. There is nothing more cleansing than grace!

Many years ago I hurt someone's feelings for no other reason but my immaturity and selfishness. For years that action haunted me. Twenty years later I tracked down this person, who lived hundreds of miles away. I called her on the phone and explained I had carried the pain of my action for too long and needed to tell her I was sorry. She laughed and said she had down far worse to others and had forgotten what I had done soon after it happened.

Why did I hang on to something that was useless for me to keep carrying for so long? In my confession and her forgiveness, a weight was lifted, and something hanging in my unconscious was finally hauled away. That is precisely what God's loving purpose and sacrifice for us is all about—so that we might unburden our souls and have our spirits returned, renewed, and full of peace.

Don't wait for once a year or for too many years to say you are sorry or to surrender to God what is only taking up space and causing you sleepless nights and guilty living. When you are ready, let go. And when you aren't ready, think about it and let go anyway! Surrender what you don't need and quit worrying about what others think about your discards. Over and over again, Jesus taught that what was in the past didn't need to color the future. Forgiveness means surrender, and grace means that God hauls off what we can't let go of. In such grace we discover the freedom of true peace!

ROBIN NEST

I WAS HAVING A PARTICULARLY stressful month. Nothing happened that hadn't happened to all of you and everyone around us. But sometimes when unexpected moments of pain, frustration, and loss come all at once, it is like being caught in a hailstorm with nowhere to hide.

Like I said, we had all been there. I was stressed. I had reacted poorly in some moments and superbly in others, but I was just worn out and needed no more. I felt overburdened and was not paying attention as I began to leave the house. You know what that feels like! This was simply to set the stage for what came next.

I was heading out of our laundry room into the garage to head back into the fray. I hit the garage door opener. As the door started to lift, the garage was still quite dark. Suddenly shadow passed over my head! I saw nothing but a dark shape with wings but was certain it was a hawk or something bigger. I was frozen, not knowing what had swooped over me and whether it was coming back to carry me away! Don't laugh; in that split moment of surprise when your mind has been elsewhere, you have all sorts of weird thoughts.

As the garage door opened all the way, I saw the culprit—a robin! It was flying back and forth and obviously didn't want me to move into the garage. It flew outside, and then I saw on top of the garage door opener a pile of sticks and straw. It had been building a nest. My next dilemma was trying to decide whether I should leave it. I was not in the mood to do anything to affect the life of even a bird. Would I have to leave the nest and be attacked every day until eggs hatched, or would there be a way to do something else? The robin flew away, so I got my ladder and checked out the nest.

Great news! It was empty and not even halfway built. I carried it outside and put it on top of the outside garage door light. I realized the robin had done all that work in less than twenty minutes, for that was the amount of time the door had been opened earlier in the day. So he could either continue where I put it or start over somewhere else. Crisis averted! And I could relax!

So here is the point: when I start feeling sorry for myself, no matter what comes next, it will likely seem more dramatic than it really is. I had had birds protecting a nest swoop at me before, but this was the first time I thought a robin was a hawk or some prehistoric flying dinosaur! Stress and fear can heighten our emotions and create tension that only magnifies any surprise or distraction.

That robin wasn't there for me, but it helped me realize it was time to take a deep breath, say a prayer, and ask for God to help me back into a place of peace. I obviously was overstressed, or a little bird wouldn't have seemed so ominous. Because I was preoccupied, I was ripe for the moment. Like an angel swooping down to bring peace, this outside help actually helped me return to the real world and settle down.

Sometimes the help we need comes from surprising places. After several incredibly emotional weeks, I was overwhelmed and had allowed stress to wind me up as tight as a spring without even realizing it. And then the gift of a robin just being a robin helped wake me up. A laugh, a short prayer, and the realization that it was time to settle down all were in order. And for a while, there again was peace in the valley.

The commandment about not having any other gods is not just about worshipping idols but also about letting anything, anyone, or any moment have more power in our lives than the peace of knowing God is with us and will bring the healing, hope, and peace that allow us to face every moment with the assurance and calmness of faith.

For a few moments, as what happens too often for all of us, I let stuff overwhelm and become the focus of my life. It took a robin to wake me up to that fact. And I am glad that it did!

WHAT DO I BELIEVE?

IT WAS TEN MONTHS SINCE my wife's death, and this was my first Easter since that devastating moment of loss. I prepared to lead worship as I always had except this was no usual Easter. Suddenly, at the altar, getting ready for the prayers, I was overwhelmed with one thought. *Do I believe what I say I believe?*

I had never thought about it that way. I had always believed that God came to earth to conquer death and that Christmas and Easter had changed reality for all time. But this was the first time Easter was up close and personal as it had never been before. As I stood at the altar, ready to lead prayers and celebrate Holy Communion, I realized I really needed to believe. That thought wouldn't leave my mind even as I began to speak. Did I believe what I always said and felt I believed?

Either Easter was the only way to not be swallowed up by death or I was about to fall into a deep pit. I silently asked God for help! If Easter was not real for me, it was time to walk away. I had never doubted, yet it struck me that if Easter isn't real, faith isn't real, and nothing makes sense at all. If that is the case, I cannot be a pastor. For a moment, time stood still. I am always amazed how quickly the mind can process so much at once, and what seemed like minutes of consideration likely happened in a split second or two, but I was in turmoil. All I could do was ask God to help me.

There is no way to explain how or why, but in that moment I felt the rush of an incredible feeling of peace. I was ready. I was sure. Easter had indeed changed my life! There was a wonderful story in Mark's Gospel of a similar moment when a father whose son was terribly sick came for healing. He wanted Jesus to heal his son, and Jesus told him faith was the source of any healing. The man said he believed but needed help with what was tough to believe. I imagine that was my prayer that morning, just as it has been for many of you. I had been so busy wrestling with grief, serving a congregation, and taking care of my kids that I hadn't stopped to allow the power of an empty tomb to bring me the joy it deserved.

This would be the most meaningful Easter ever! It was the first time I had to really face a tomb and be assured death is not the end. Every Easter should be a time for us to face the reality of what we believe! It was the only festival of the early church as the resurrection of the Messiah is the only reason there is to follow Christ!

God has changed our lives, and we need to take time to allow that fact to truly change our lives. Easter is the moment of all moments. Never take it for granted or just go through the motions. I speak from experience. Don't be afraid to ask God for the same gift a father asked Jesus when he said he did believe but needed help with what was hard to believe. When we let go of what we cannot comprehend, God blesses us with the peace that is beyond the world's understanding. It is all about God's gifts to us and accepting what God alone can bring to pass. Faith is not about understanding but about believing.

A GRANDMA'S LOVE

MY GRANDMA WAS MORE SPECIAL than I realized when I was too young to understand. I always loved her and couldn't wait for our annual vacation visit, but I never really understood her.

Her cooking was awesome, and I could still imagine the aroma of her coffee cakes. I'd never forget her incredible fried chicken or the mashed potatoes and gravy that were part of the deal. Her canned fruit, jams, and jellies were out of this world. It seems as if she was always in the kitchen or taking clothes from the washing machine to hang them out in the backyard to dry. But here is one memory I find terribly embarrassing.

She never forgot a birthday or a holiday. But I gradually became aware of a pattern. Every Valentine's, birthday, or special occasion card had something in common. Under the greeting inside the card was a piece of masking tape on which she would write, "Love, Grandpa and Grandma." I never figured out why she wrote on tape, until one year I decided on some detective work and peeled back the tape.

To my amazement there was someone else's name on the card that the tape covered up. The next time a card arrived, I did the same thing and found a different name. And then it dawned on me that Grandma was sending used cards. She was recycling before I had even heard such a word. Even though there was usually a dollar bill with the card, from that time on, I always felt cheated and felt Grandma was being cheap. Boy, did I have a lot to learn!

Over time as I grasped the realities of her life, I grew to understand. She had endured World Wars I and II, the Great Depression, and epidemics of polio and influenza. Grandpa didn't make much money, and she spent all her time making clothes for her children, canning fruit and vegetables for meals, and feeding pigeons in their coop, which were sold or bartered for doctor visits and necessary groceries. Grandma survived on very little and learned to repurpose before that became a red badge of courage for the educated and affluent.

What a clueless child I was! How embarrassing it is today to admit how judgmental, even as a little kid, I had been. What I missed then was that she loved us so much she made certain we had a special contact from her at important times of the year. She couldn't afford long-distance phone calls or new cards from Hallmark but never missed an opportunity to let each of us know we were loved by her!

Because we lived so far away, we only saw our grandparents once a year. But our times with Grandma and Grandpa were some of the best memories of all, and I would give anything to give Grandma one more hug today. Now I understand her effort to go out of her way to touch my life (even if I wasn't smart enough yet to appreciate her love). Such love is a gift I will never forget. She couldn't afford much, but she never held back when it came to love! God touches us in so many ways. It is just that sometimes it takes a while for us to realize the power of his love.

WILD TURKEYS

AS CHRISTMAS CAME CLOSER, THERE was a distraction of surprise visitors we hadn't seen in some time. It was our little flock of wild turkeys, which lived in the forest behind our church building. While everyone's attention and concerns were with getting ready for Christmas, the surprise entrance into our parking lot of wild turkeys changed our focus. For a moment the spotlight was on turkeys and not a baby in a manger; they became impossible to ignore.

Turkeys in the wild are interesting critters. I am relatively certain they have some plan of action, but watching them makes one wonder. They wander around, constantly changing direction. *Slow* and *uninspired* are the two words I will use to describe their wandering.

As I watched them moving from door to door as they inspected our building, I assumed they were on the prowl for food but either didn't know where to look or were easily distracted by reflections of ground-level windows (even stopping to peck at their reflections). Mostly they dawdled, which was an art form they had mastered.

At that moment they brought to mind a contrasting vision of a familiar Christmas theme, which was the account of wise men searching for Jesus. While turkeys wandered, those visitors from far away had a much clearer pathway in mind. While turkeys seemed clueless and disgraced, those ancient visitors from the east knew exactly what they were looking for and had a plan for how their search might be rewarded.

As I focused on such contrasts, it also came to mind that we live surrounded by a world full of people who fit into one of those two categories. Either they have seen God's light and follow its glow or they mindlessly wander, looking for what satisfies, being easily distracted by reflections and shiny things.

During the darkness of winter, in a world darkened by the infections of sin that surround us, even a little light goes a long way. If focused on the real reason for the season, the light of a manger is enough to bring a smile to every face and joy to every heart. On the other hand, dazzling offers, pop-up ads, and tempting promises can distract and keep people from the only peace that calms every trouble and brings joy to any heart.

January 6 is the last day of Christmas and remembers the visit of the wise ones, led on their journey by a light missed by much of the world. Contrasting their vision with the mindless meanderings of goofy turkeys, we are reminded of our daily choices. Most living boils down to only two options. One is following the light of God's love, while the other is beginning while distracted by the dull reflections of a broken world.

Don't ever forget the joy and excitement of the Bethlehem birth. Be assured as well that if Jesus is the glow in your eyes, others will see his light and be touched by the same joy and peace. There is nothing wrong with dawdling and wandering once in a while, but having seen the true light, how can we not let it lead and guide us with the confident hope and peaceful joy it alone can bring?

TATTOOS

WHEN I WAS A CHILD, the only tattoos I ever noticed were on the arms of sailors or in the pages of *National Geographic*. As has always been the case, change is constant. I bring up tattoos only as an element of the story that follows. Today I don't pay much attention to tattoos as they are everywhere, but there was a time when any tattoo was noticeable and unique.

While attending the seminary, I worked as a bank teller to earn enough to pay my tuition. In doing so, I also gained a practical education about life. I met many people from different cultures and walks of life and with incredibly unique backgrounds. This became a supplemental education, often more practical and helpful than some of my classwork. It was helpful to be in contact with such a variety of people I never would have encountered had I spent all my time on the seminary campus, surrounded by guys who were going to become pastors.

One of my regular customers was a retired gentleman from a department store called Famous-Barr. He sold and tailored suits for much of his life. He had a European accent and always wore long-sleeved white shirts and a suit coat even on the hottest, most humid of Saint Louis summer days. One day he came to my window to deposit his social security check. His sleeve got caught on the edge of my teller window and slid all the way up to his elbow.

In that brief moment, I noticed he had a tattoo I had never seen! It was a series of blue numbers on his forearm. I couldn't miss them, and then it hit me! He had survived the horror of a Nazi concentration camp!

I quickly looked away, hoping he hadn't realized what I saw. There was no way I would have asked any question about what was so unspeakable, but I would never forget that tattoo. Even worse was the reminder it must have been for him every day of his life.

So there are tattoos, but there are also indelible images and memories each of us carries in our lives we would rather forget. To ease such burdens, we may find ways to share what we can't forget with someone we love or trust. Some burdens should never be carried alone. Others we will never admit and do all we can to forget, but they never go away as we can't change the past.

However, there is a love that is stronger than anything we seek to hide or try to forget. It is God's word of mercy and forgiveness. Our mistakes and unforgettable images from the past are impossible to erase. Yet the miracle of Calvary is that Jesus has made them part of his body and buried them in his tomb. His victory on Easter announces there is no burden we need carry alone. There is no pain or mistake he is not willing to forgive and forget.

In baptism, we are not tattooed, but an invisible sign of the cross is made over us. That image is the reminder of God's love and the price that has been paid for our gifts of healing, hope, and peace. Every time we see the image of the cross, we remember what should never be hidden or forgotten, which is the healing love of God and the incredible love that has changed who we are.

A SLOW START

WHEN I GRADUATED FROM THE seminary in May, I was ready to be a pastor. I had met all the classroom requirements and was ready be set loose in some congregation. But there were not enough churches anxious for a rookie to break into the starting lineup.

I had worked in a bank throughout the seminary years, and by September, I was certain I would be in that bank for the next twenty years. I interviewed with two churches, but neither offered me a call. I was disappointed. Surely, any church was better than none at all. Gradually my focus shifted as I considered a career in banking. I was disappointed as it seemed eight years of college and seminary education were all in vain. There was no doubt God would take care of me, but what I wanted was not what I was getting.

To say those months became a lesson in patience was an understatement. Early in October, however, the seminary's director of placement told me my name was given to a congregation in Toledo for a possible one-year contract. The pastor was taking a year of leave of absence for graduate work. They wanted someone to fill in for that year. Such an offer was unheard of as graduates usually were called to serve in a congregation but never for only one year!

I could not conceive of going to a town with no guarantee and having to go through the process all over again with no job at all. My wife and I talked and prayed about the idea of giving up our jobs and moving to Toledo for only one year and then having no idea what would come next. On the Friday of the week, I called the placement office and said I was not interested. I resolved to stay working at the bank and accepted that as my possible near-term career.

On Monday the placement director called me at work and said he called the congregation about my desire to be off the list. In that conversation he was told they had a call meeting the day before and had called me for that one-year position, not knowing of my desire to be taken out of consideration. Then I received a call from the district president, who told me I had to take the call. Then the pastor who was leaving for a year called and told me I had received a divine call and should prayerfully consider coming to Toledo. Everyone was telling me that I should accept this divine call I had decided I would not consider. To say I was confused and pressured was another understatement. I didn't know what to do and was frustrated by all the pressure, already having decided this was not worthy of even considering.

After a week of prayer and conversation with my wife, we finally decided maybe God had a hand in this and it was worthy of a positive response. My sole reason for sharing this was to say we had a remarkable ten years in that congregation, made lifelong friends, had a successful ministry, and added three children into our home. And that prepared me for my next congregation, which I served for almost forty years. But what an incredible series of events that led to all this!

I don't believe God has been pulling all the strings, but there is no doubt in my mind God is with us in every moment and decision we have made. His blessing touches so many parts of my life as is the same for you. Sometimes faith is more about trusting what we can't see than assuming our vision and wisdom is as good as God's. Faith does work.

ROUGH FLIGHT TO IRELAND

ROXANNE AND I PLANNED AND waited for a vacation to Ireland. It would be our first trip out of the country, and it was a time of nervous excitement. And yet we had a rough beginning to that dream trip as we endured the most uncomfortable plane ride ever.

It began as we waited an extra hour before they could find a jet for our flight. At last, one arrived at our gate, and we were allowed to board. As we finally got into our seats, we noticed it was not what we expected as a typical wide-bodied jet to cross the Atlantic. It was a smaller jet typical of those used for cross-country flights with only three seats on each side of the aisle and only two restrooms in the rear.

Before takeoff, the front door was reopened. The pilot announced we didn't have enough fuel to cross the Atlantic and must wait for additional fuel. Then the smell of aviation fuel filled the cabin! Thirty minutes later the doors were closed. We then sat and waited forty-five minutes to leave as we had lost our place in line for a runway. We finally took off for an eight-hour flight. For the first hour, all we could smell was the lingering odor of aviation fuel.

The flight was full, so the serving cart was in the center aisle for almost the entire trip. It was impossible to stand or stretch. There was only one chance to run to the restroom. There were no monitors for distraction, the cabin was too warm, and it was impossible to budge even an inch in our seats. More than once I wondered if we had made a mistake getting on this flight and couldn't understand why we were in such a cramped plane for such a long flight. Finally, when it seemed as if the nightmare would never end, we started our descent into Ireland.

As we looked out in the early light of dawn, we could see the Shannon River, green pastures, an old castle, small houses, rock walls, and flocks of sheep. It was a beautiful sight as the sun was beginning to rise. We landed and finally were out of the jet and ready for our experience in Ireland, which turned into one of the most fulfilling and enjoyable vacations ever!

The uncomfortableness of that flight was an instant and distant memory. It didn't matter anymore! Life is often like that. So often, the things that seem overwhelming and unexpected become like small potatoes compared with the joy that follows. It is the same with the promises of faith. So often in the New Testament letters of Paul, he reminds his readers that the pain and disappointments of today will pale in comparison. The present never lasts forever. Our trip to Ireland is an object lesson of exactly what that all means.

In God's hands there is far more than meets the eye. What we see today will be gone tomorrow. And the gifts we cannot yet see will last forever. Faith truly can change our perspective.

GERMAN LESSONS

YEARS AGO WE VISITED MY brother and his wife when they were living in Germany. He was in the army, as my father had been. We lived there for three years when I was in grade school, and this was the first time I had an opportunity to return to some of our old haunts. We took several road trips during the week we were there.

One excursion was to the wonderful region of Bavaria. That part of Germany was more traditional, less urbanized, and filled with mountains, heavy forests, and the rich heritage of the past. Cuckoo clock makers, wood carvers, and hillside farms were everywhere. The pace was slower, and the past hadn't been changed as much as in the big cities. The land was hilly and full of dark forests and wonderful green pastures. So many memories returned as we had often vacationed in that region many years before.

In the newer urban regions and cities like Frankfurt or Cologne, it was easy to find people who could speak English. (How embarrassing to realize that in other countries, almost everyone speaks at least two languages, if not three, with one usually English. For us, this is not often the case, but that is a subject for another time.) Anyway, our menu was only in German, and I had no clue what most of the food items were.

As was typical in the older, more traditional towns, a small hotel would have a restaurant. There were not many tables, so people were seated wherever there was room. We were escorted to a table where an older man in a suit was already eating his meal. As we picked up the menus, written entirely in German, we began a quiet conversation with each other as we tried to figure out what we would eat. We almost whispered, mostly out of embarrassment, as even my brother, who spoke passable German, was having difficulty reading the menu. For some reason, we were concerned the gentleman across from us might think we were tourists or something. (Ha! As if he couldn't tell!)

My brother finally figured out enough, and after sharing what he thought was on the menu, he ordered for all of us. He was also careful to order a vegetarian entrée he was certain his wife would appreciate. When we were done, wondering how to carry on a conversation with someone else so close, the gentleman seated at our table looked at us and with a distinctively Southern drawl asked, "Y'all American?"

We started laughing as he gave us grief for our attempt to hide our language difficulties. As it turned out, he worked for the State Department, and we had a delightful visit. He finished his meal and left just as our food arrived.

We were in for another surprise. Three of us got what we anticipated, but my sister-in-law's order was not what my brother expected! It was a platter full of every vegetable imaginable, probably about ten pounds' worth, and obviously meant as a dish for an entire family to share. We got a charge out of that, and I learned several things that evening.

One reminder is that it is better to admit what we don't know and not be embarrassed to ask for help. Another lesson to consider is how helpful it will be to learn at least some of the language of others than expect it as their responsibility to learn ours. A final lesson is that it is a good idea never to make assumptions about strangers but instead to simply reach out and find out who your neighbor really is. There is so much that we have learned on that one memorable night!

GRANDPARENTS

MY GRANDPARENTS LIVED IN SAINT Joseph, Missouri. Grandpa was manager of a seed warehouse. Grandma was a full-time mother and active volunteer at church. We saw them once a year, and I loved to go fishing with Grandpa. Grandma's fried chicken and fruit pies were incredible!

Our best times were when Grandpa would take us to the seed house on Saturdays. It was a four-story brick warehouse with wood floors and an open elevator. Burlap bags of grass seed were stacked floor to ceiling everywhere! There is no way to describe the smell of so much burlap, alfalfa, rye, and other grasses, but I remember the aroma even to this day.

During the Depression years, my grandparents survived on the pigeons they raised in a little coop in the backyard, their little garden, and fruit trees that provided canned fruit for the winter. They bartered for doctor visits with pigeons or canned goods. We loved to visit and hide in the pigeon coop or fight for turns on the wooden swing on their front porch. They had a tiny attic full of boxes of toys and books from when my dad was a little kid, and we could never get enough of being in that house.

My grandparents were two of the happiest, most loving people I had ever known, and I thought they were the richest people on the earth. Years later, I realized how they struggled to get by on so little. Grandma always worked in the home. Grandpa didn't make that much money from the seed house. When we retired, he had social security but no pension. Medicaid took care of their last years in a nursing home along with help from their kids. Grandpa died first. After Grandma's funeral, something happened that I would never forget.

Dad announced each grandchild had a gift from their grandparents. As he had been closing his parents' bank accounts, he found they had a safe-deposit box and was surprised by what was in it. Whenever a grandchild was born, Grandpa bought a $50 savings bond in the name of that child. Dad found those and decided that as we gathered for a meal after Grandma's funeral, it was a good time for him to share their gifts with all of us.

At the time, I thought that it wasn't very much. Over the years, I had come to understand something I was too young and selfish at the time to figure out. For people who had so little, even the meager amount it took to buy each savings bond was an incredible sacrifice of love. And over time, with that appreciation, the reality of their sacrifice made such a gift more valuable than any monetary value. Such love, which was taught to them by the example of Jesus, cannot be measured or valued as we do other things.

My grandparents' faith and willingness to love has been one of the greatest blessings of my life and continues to bring tears to my eyes even today. I am blessed beyond what I deserve, but such is grace and how it changes lives. I did not cash in that bond for many years, and its value increased much more than its face value, but more than that, it was the loving sacrifice of that gift that I would never forget. What a special lesson they have taught me about what it means to love and how easy it is to share such a love in daily and many ways.

LOSSES AND GAINS

WE ALL DEAL WITH LOSSES, beginning from the moment we leave the comfort of the womb. Some are minor, while many are major. The only consistency with loss is there is no undo switch. And with any loss, our reactions range from surprise to disappointment or unrestrained grief.

Loss obviously means that something we've had our hands on or has been near has disappeared. We all deal with having things taken away or having to be surrendered, and usually that is to something we wish to deal with. Over time, however, I have learned that losses can also add more than we realize at first blush.

My firstborn was a joy-filled, curly haired bundle of energy. Soon after college, she married and had a baby. Our first grandchild was only a year old when her mother, our daughter, died. I was devastated and didn't even know how to feel, even though my wife had died a few years earlier. Losing a child is something no parent ever expects.

After her death, I would never forget another father, who had lost a daughter to death, telling me, "Welcome to the fraternity no one wants to join." Before them, I only knew him in passing. His words were not negative but an invitation to allow his journey from grief to healing to be a gift to me, at a time when I hurt more than I ever did. Over time, he and others had shared what had been gained in their losses to help me deal with mine. That was possible only through the power of faith in their lives.

There is so much about God's love we take for granted when we think we have it all. But in times of loss, we are lifted to new plateaus of faith with the reminder Jesus's purpose is to embrace our losses, make them his own, and bring healing and hope none of us deserve or expect. So often, the words of scripture remind us that our earthly blessings are nothing compared with the love of God. Saint Paul often wrote about how willing he was to surrender everything and anything in order that his gifts from God would become his only focus.

Such thoughts speak to all of us as we learn to lose the stranglehold of grief or the unanswerable questions we continue to ask. In being reminded that Christ's love is precisely for such losses in our lives, I became better at understanding how his hope and peace were added to my life in a fullness I had never understood before. My daughter did not die so I would learn a lesson, but Christ died for me so I would understand that his love was to overcome my daughter's death and my parental grief.

We can lament our losses, or we can color and heal them with the gain of a loving God who offers unlimited love, healing, and peace that the world is unable to share. Losses will always hurt and change us, but the change of faith turns loss into a gain! Another father taught me that in opening his loss, he changed mine!

DECEPTIONS

A NATIONAL NEWSPAPER PRINTED A provocative headline stating that a prominent bronze plaque at the US Military Academy featured a hooded member of the Ku Klux Klan. In our culture of heightened guilt and sensitivity about the past, such headlines could be more damaging than the facts that followed. Because my father and brother were West Point graduates, and we had lived on the academy for three years when I was in middle school, I had strong ties to that place, and the idea that this was a prominent part of the history of the academy, as the newspaper article insinuated, was a surprise that caught me off guard.

I recently visited the academy and made certain to find that bronze plaque. I was surprised to find that the image was one of a series of three bronze relief castings that were each eleven feet high and five feet wide. Each panel depicted various moments in the history of this nation's growth. The image mentioned in the newspaper headline was only about three by four inches and was located on the bottom corner of one of the three massive bronze plaques that were full of hundreds of images, most of which were much larger.

This small image was part of the painful reality of a broken world and a fact of our history, which included the best and worst of who we are. Anyone who didn't read the full story or see these panels firsthand would make incorrect assumptions about West Point. The headline had been intentionally provocative and objectively misleading. It was deceptive and disappointing.

How often have we made assumptions based on misleading words or incomplete information? A partial truth can only lead to mistaken and disturbing reactions. When we are so trusting of a source, we can't consider any agenda or motives behind what is shared. We see this daily in advertising, political ads, internet tweets and posts, or gossip that is embellished as it passes from person to person. As children of God, our call is to filter life through the gift of God's grace rather than fanning the flames or stirring the pot. That was the point of Genesis, as a serpent shared half-truths that led Adam and Eve to decisions from which they couldn't recover.

One law from Sinai is about bearing a false witness or, in other words, telling the whole truth. There is a danger in truth that is not complete and lies that are meant to deceive. Such efforts bring devastating consequences, often introducing pain, distress, and hardship into innocent lives. There is a reason Jesus has spent so much time teaching about love and forgiveness rather than seeking only to hurt or destroy anytime we feel we have been harmed. Consider how often we have heard that something is the gospel truth yet has nothing to do with the Gospel or with complete and honest truth.

We can do better! Be careful with what you say. Be careful with what you hear. Gossip and half-truths are tempting but always leave a bitter aftertaste. Just because something is tempting doesn't mean it is true. Life is difficult enough; why ever go out of your way to make it even more so? For people of God, there is always a better way!

ALARM

YEARS AGO WHEN I COULD still carry my youngest daughter, Abby, in a backpack, I took her to the zoo. It was a typical Friday adventure for us. That was my day off, which I often tried to use as an opportunity to take her someplace different. She was never at a loss for questions, comments, or explorations. She was only two years old at the time, small enough to carry and old enough to engage in a conversation (of sorts).

This trip to the zoo took place on a hot and humid summer morning. We finally arrived at the penguin house, which was air-conditioned and a wonderful relief from the weather outside. The penguins were always fun to watch, even more so with the air-conditioning and respite from the heat. When we had seen enough, we headed toward the exit and the heat that awaited us outside.

Just as we were ready to leave, I heard the rumble of thunder and saw a flash of lightning, and a sudden downpour followed. We had just gotten to the exit, which was surrounded by glass windows. We could see how intense the storm was and could tell it would be a while before we could go outside. With many others, we stood by the doors, waiting for the storm to pass. When it finally stopped, I started to move but was stopped in my tracks when the fire alarms went off.

My first thought was to wonder how there could be a fire in a building full of aquariums and water. We were surrounded by the noise of sirens, and emergency strobe lights were flashing all around us. A first impulse was to run outside, but the storm wasn't letting up. Then I remembered I had someone little in a backpack and turned around to make certain Abby wasn't panicked by the noise. She wasn't.

Then I saw it! The alarm pull was right behind me, next to Abby and the backpack. I had a funny feeling that I knew who could have pulled the alarm, as little hands are always in motion and exploring. I had leaned right next to an alarm without even thinking about that. Now what? Had anyone noticed? What should I do?

The only response that made sense to me was to casually follow the crowd outside and move as far away from that building as I could. I didn't know for certain whether she pulled the alarm. I did know she was too young to be handcuffed and questioned. But my heart was thumping so hard I was sure others could hear it! Even if she had pulled that alarm, nothing would change other than a lecture and embarrassment for me.

Surprises are always followed by panic or pain, embarrassment or overreaction. This was a nonconsequential moment, yet it was filled with anxiety. Surprises bring unplanned responses. We react without forethought. And we do the best we can with the facts at hand. We can never be prepared for what we can't anticipate, so what is the point of worry or guilt? Life will always be full of surprises, but forgiveness and God's presence are always on the table. With such gifts assured, faith guarantees there is nothing we cannot handle and we'll always have help when we worry needlessly!

UNMASKING GRACE

WHEN THE COVID-19 RESTRICTIONS WERE removed, we all had to deal with the freedom of being unmasked. It was interesting that something we all complained about for so long was responded to with some hesitancy. What we were so used to and understood to be protective became unnecessary for most. Everyone was confused as different locales had different rules. While masks were unnecessary in most settings, some businesses said they were still necessary for the unvaccinated. In other places, such as hospitals, everyone still had to wear a mask.

I do not want to debate the science. I want to focus on behavior to make a bigger point. Think for a moment how something we didn't like to do became so much a part of our routine that (even with being vaccinated) it was a little difficult to adapt to a new behavior. Here is the bottom line: We never wore masks until we had to. We debated, but we wore them. We weren't comfortable with them but got used to a new behavior. And now that we have been set free, many are not sure how to act.

In some ways it is like guilt and grace. When we do what we shouldn't do, we try to hide it. When we fear being judged as guilty, we try to mask our discomfort and hide in any way that we can. It is like a little white lie that leads to a different little lie to cover the first one and then more after that. Over time, we even find ways to convince ourselves the mistakes we have made aren't really that bad. Sometimes we try to convince ourselves they have never happened. As we run, hide, or make excuses, it is like wearing a mask to keep others from seeing the truth of our imperfect lives.

It is an attempt at protecting ourselves from any punishment or disclosure that can embarrass or hurt us.

Such is life. Sin covers what is good and seeks to hide what is wrong and hurtful. God's grace is an unmasking and the promise of freedom from the burdens of guilt. It removes the self-protective masks we've thought so necessary and have gotten so used to. Jesus carries our disturbing actions and moments away, creating a new life changed by the undeserved gifts powered by the cross and empty tomb. Forgiveness uncovers and erases guilt, period! But it is difficult for us to live as free people. We have hidden for so long that we fear such a gift is too good to be true. We are tempted to keep some protection around just in case. We want to be forgiven but on our terms and under our control.

It takes trust to live as forgiven people because we must first admit the need for forgiveness. It takes courage to be honest to one another about who we really are and where we have been. One can't accept the gift of grace without first being honest about the fact that only God's love can set us free. And we need to take off the mask forever if we are to live as free people.

Here is how it works too often for me: I want to be free from sin, but there are some things I want to pretend I really haven't done, and I worry that someday someone may find out. So I keep spare masks around to cover up or hide, just in case I need them. The gift of Jesus's grace calls me to be honest with myself and God about how far I often fall and then to celebrate how lovingly God holds on tight and lifts me no matter what.

After my wife's death, I had such difficulty dealing with my grief and wasn't the best dad my daughter needed and deserved. I was so selfishly overwhelmed with my pain that I was unable to understand hers. I missed opportunities I had learned over the years to handle better now than I did then. I would still rather keep a mask on this guilt, which is embarrassing to remember or admit. But if I truly believe in the wonderful, undeserved love Jesus offers, shouldn't I celebrate such a gift and quit covering up what God promises has been forgiven? Why do I need to fear being discovered or fail to admit that I have made some mistakes? How much better it is to accept what has been given out of love and learn to share that same love much better tomorrow than I may have yesterday?

If I am forgiven before I have even been born, that really does mean

God's love is stronger than my weakness! If I repent (which is all John the Baptist was asking for at the Jordan River), then I am standing in the same river of grace in which Jesus stands. How about just understanding that *repent* simply means to take off the mask and believe you don't need to wear it anymore? Is that not a wonderful example and understanding of what grace truly entails?

So maybe our months of wrestling with masks and then being told to take them off can be a great object lesson for us to understand what Jesus keeps trying to convince us to believe when he shares his love, forgives our sins, and calls us to live unburdened by the heavy burdens he has lifted off our backs. Forgiveness means it is OK to pitch the mask and learn the joy of being free!

TELEVISION WESTERNS

WE OFTEN WONDER WHY GOD allows unfair and undeserved hardship and pain. It is confusing when bad things happen especially to good or innocent people. People without faith claim such moments prove there is no God. We often treat faith like a vaccine that will prevent anything harmful, painful, or unfair.

Recently I stumbled across a favorite Western of the 1950s called *The Rifleman*. The main character was a Civil War veteran and widower. He moved from Virginia with his ten-year-old son to New Mexico to begin a new life. They bought a farmhouse and land and were ready for the good life until some tough guys burned the house down and tried to steal their land. The son asked why God had brought them all this way, only to let them down. His tears as he cried to his father mirrored many of our similar prayers to God.

Many shows of that era contained a moral lesson, and good usually triumphed over evil. I was engrossed and totally caught off guard when the dad, who was a crack shot with a rifle, decided to tell his son a story rather than shoot the bad guys. He told his son about a rancher from another part of the world, thousands of years ago, whose beard reached all the way to his feet. His name was Job. He loved God and was a good guy. But the devil told God that Job had faith only because his life was so easy. God told the devil he was wrong and nothing he could do would change the goodness of Job. The devil killed Job's family, destroyed all his crops, and stole his herd of cattle. Job said they were wrong. The next lines blew me away.

Job's friends said God must be punishing him, or else this never would have happened. The father then quoted a Bible passage in which Job said that no matter what evil came his way, he knew that his Redeemer would triumph in the end. This show had its share of violence we would find so improper today but also shared that lesson.

The son said he guessed they really didn't have it so bad after all. And of course, the story proceeded with the dad confronting the bad guys, who wound up rebuilding the man's house rather than get in trouble with the law. It was a standard 1950s Western, and I was amazed at how a Western became a vehicle to retell a Bible story that was accurately quoted. That episode showed a son learning a life lesson from, of all places, the Bible.

Our world today is no different from the 1950s. Sin just reveals itself in new ways, and our reaction has even more possibilities available for a response. But our culture is different in other ways, which is why I am amazed to hear a biblical message in a completely natural and normal way. This isn't a religious show, yet everyone seems comfortable with a biblical message.

In our culture of heightened sensitivities and political correctness, such a reference to scripture is no longer standard fare. And I've realized how quiet many of us are about what we believe. We will stand up for a political cause or a secular movement but often don't have a similar passion (in public) to share our faith, especially if we fear being criticized or misunderstood or associated with others who misuse the biblical message for reasons other than what it is intended.

I was in high school when Vietnam protests were in full bloom. My classmates often asked how my father, as a Christian, could be part of the US Army. (It usually was phrased in a much meaner way.) My standard reply was, "What better place for a Christian to be than in the army?" And I would have said the same thing no matter what profession he was in. If we are to be a light to the world, we need to be in the world and simply live what we believe. That is how we make a difference, and that is how the light shines.

My dad's battalion in Vietnam was camped in the jungle on Christmas Eve. I still have a copy of the message he passed around to his commanders and platoon leaders saying he hoped the real message of that night would be a comfort and bring peace to his troops who were separated from family and friends. He could not have put that in writing today, but I know he would have still told his troops that Christmas Eve was God's response to a broken world. He was like that. And he was never embarrassed about who he was.

We face the same problems today that the world has faced in the 1950s or during the time of Job. Anger, fear, bitterness, illness, and death break us to pieces. But God's gift to the world is the good news that he has a plan to restore what has been broken and to repair what has been lost. There are so many ways we live differently because of that news and share what we know to be true. We can complain about how difficult it is to be a Christian in our world today, or faith can help us believe that because our Redeemer lives, we shall live also, and nothing can separate us from God's love. If a television character can be seen as making sure his son knows right from wrong in such a way, I think each of us can find ways to do the same. Our children, our neighbors, and God's children in every part of the world deserve such love. And it starts with us. Don't be afraid to let the light shine, especially when we see how dark the shadows around us can be!

GRIEF

WHEN OUR BEAGLE NAMED WINSTON died, we were devastated! He was definitely special and different from the other dogs we had known and loved. He was a rescue dog from Kentucky and had issues. He was a rescue from the SPCA. He had crooked teeth and a notch in his left ear, was afraid of every noise, and most likely had been abused as a puppy. But he became central to our life as a family.

We have all experienced losses of loved ones, which are certainly more difficult than losing a pet. But it is amazing how close we get to our pets and how intense our grief at their loss can be. Sometimes they are more loving, accepting, and civilized than many people we encounter.

Winston never barked but in the past few years learned to howl like a beagle, and that was his welcome to us as we pulled into the garage. A week after his death, I came downstairs in the morning and was sure that I heard him shaking his head and the familiar sound of his ears flopping. I knew he wasn't there but knew I heard that sound. That evening when I pulled into the garage, I was certain I heard his howl. I am overwhelmed with the complexity of our brain and memory and how we are conditioned in certain situations to expect certain results. At the same time, this always catches me off guard.

When my first wife died, I was once watching our kids play soccer and saw someone across the field I was sure was my wife! Familiar posture, familiar hair, familiar jacket, and yet I knew it couldn't be her. But memories can do that to us, and we have no control for a moment or two, until reason returns. But central to dealing with grief is learning to let go.

The only problem is that sometimes the wrestling match going on in our brain won't let it happen.

Losses and grief are complicated, and each of us deals with them in different ways and time frames. The more we care and love, the more difficult loss is and the more intense grief can be. Even though our rational and reasoning mind can be realistic, our subconscious and unconscious can trigger familiar smells, sounds, and sights that catch us off guard. The bottom line is we don't like to let go of what we don't want to, and sometimes even when we know we must, there are triggers that get in the way. I get it.

Well, here is another moment to share. Winston never did learn to chew on really big bones. He would bury them, and we never saw them again. Last week one of his bones showed up on our back deck. It was covered with mud and had been carried and deposited on the deck. Was that a *Twilight Zone* moment or just a weird coincidence? It certainly caused me to pause for a moment and wonder what was going on. It became another reminder of how much I missed that goofy, wonderful dog and how easily grief got stirred in my head and in my heart. Memories are only electrical impulses in the brain, but they are as real as what they bring to mind.

I share all this just as an example that we all can relate to. On the first Easter morning, we remember how Mary showed up at the tomb. It was empty, but that didn't change her grief or sense of loss. She knew something had changed but didn't know what. Her mind and spirit that were wrestling with grief were holding her back from celebrating something new. The tomb was empty, but that didn't register at all. Her grief and memories overpowered reality.

So full of tears were her eyes that even when Jesus stood next to her, she couldn't see who he was. Her memories of the cross and years of being with a healthy Messiah were all she could feel. Tears clouded her vision until Jesus spoke her name. And she snapped out of it. Grief became joy, and joy became her life.

We all have losses, pain, and grief in our lives, but God's love is greater, and his promises change how we look at what we think we have lost. Jesus once talked about God's care for flowers and sparrows to emphasize that if such lowly creatures are cared for by God, we certainly should know that even more love is coming our way!

The price of love is that the more we love, the more difficult our grief becomes. If it doesn't hurt, it must not have been love. And aren't those painful memories good ones that remind what has been important in our lives and what we will never forget? Will we have it any other way? As painful as memories are and the moments that trigger grief, isn't it better to know that we will never forget?

It is even better to celebrate that God will never forget us! His love is so great that he took on human skin to endure what we must all face so we would not be trapped in grief but free to celebrate the gifts of this life and the hope of the next. Memories can be painful, but the greatest reminder of the antidote to such pain is the sight of that empty tomb.

For us the bottom line is always Easter. Because of God's love and promises, grief is still grief, but it is tempered by a stronger power and hope. I should never pretend loss doesn't hurt, and it is better to have loved and lost than never to have loved at all. But even better is knowing that Jesus's "losses" (as Saint Paul says) are now my gains! Yes, sometimes it hurts to remember, but the love of God keeps even that pain in perspective.

PRAYER

FACEBOOK ONCE CONSIDERED ADDING A prayer request feature. They obviously saw this as a great public relations opportunity, but it caused me to reflect on the need many have for the support of others in their time of need, as well as the assumption that God would pay more attention to the prayers of many than only a few.

Prayer is crucial to our lives of faith and is our communication with God. However, why do we worry that God is more interested in the prayers of many than the quiet prayers of only a few? We have so many concerns and want to make certain our prayer bases are all covered.

A woman once asked for medical details about a person we prayed for in worship. I explained I couldn't reveal medical information. She testily responded, "How can I pray for her if I don't know what is wrong with her?" I understood the genuine concern but explained God knew what was wrong and wasn't dependent on our prayer to give information he already had. That seemed to calm her for a moment, but she still insisted she couldn't pray without specifics.

Years ago, conversational prayer was making a big splash in churches. Such prayers often started with the same formula: "Lord, I just want to tell you …," and specifics followed. That struck me in a strange way. The casual, conversational tone wasn't an issue, for I believe we should speak with God like a parent or a close friend. It was the feeling of intent, as if we were afraid we were a bother to God, and the more casual our approach, the less likely God would be put off by our boldness to ask.

Now why will we ever think God's love and time is more important than his love for us? Maybe I have overreacted, but the tone of such an approach doesn't seem to have the feel of a confident way of approaching a God of love. I understand the need of those who reject the formality or the formulas some think are necessary for a good and thoughtful prayer, but to approach God so timidly still strikes me as odd. It is like we are trying to make God become one of us rather than celebrate that his power and love are beyond our comprehension.

We all have times when we casually respond to a crisis in the life of another and promise that we will pray for them. And too often, we quickly move on to something else and don't follow through with actual prayer. It is almost as if our promise is enough, and we feel the offer to pray is the same as actually praying. But why hold out the promise of prayer and not follow through?

Prayer is likely our most personal connection with God. It is a special moment where we are standing on holy ground and are most likely to open ourselves to God alone. In daily living we have multiple opportunities and ways to speak honestly and lovingly with friends and family. When we trust, we open up. When we have needs, we ask. When we want to support, we share. I have read often that what sets us apart from animals is the ability to speak. Animals communicate but likely on a more basic level as the gift and nuance of language allows us to be more specific and precise, and when we aren't understood, we can try a new approach. We are used to conversation, and we are comfortable sharing thoughts, ideas, concerns, disappointments, and requests. But prayer is sometimes an enigma as we forget its power and its convenience.

When we pray at the same time every day, whether before a meal or at bedtime, such a pattern assures we will not forget to pray. At the same time, we need to pay greater attention so we are not merely racing through words without thinking, or assuming this is an action on a checklist rather than an opportunity a faith conversation offers. On the other hand, when we pray because we don't know what else to do, it may be one of our most special times as we realize God is our only hope. Such a moment is possibly one of the few times in life we truly humble ourselves before God. Too often, we assume we have all the answers and never even think about including God. When we have no choice but to pray, we are learning what it is so easy to take for granted or forget. When prayer is all we have left, it is the beginning of real answers.

Prayer is a powerful, live, real link with God. It is our moment to be honest, humble, and confident that there is nothing we may discuss, admit, or ask that God can't handle. At the same time, consider that more silence on our part in prayer will raise the possibility we may hear God's answer. Silence in prayer is more important than words, for in prayer we open ourselves to God, who knows everything already. The benefit of such a surrender is the potential to understand, perceive, or hear what God has likely been offering all along!

Maybe prayers on Facebook can be useful, but such a platform isn't private and may attract more noise than you expect. Never forget: prayer is a gift from God, not an app from a business. We do need to pray more often and become more comfortable in thanking God, asking God, and listening to God. Rather than finding easier ways for others to help us pray, simply surrendering to God is the power inherent in prayer. It seems too easy, but remember: God has done the heavy lifting already and is the One who has called us in the first place. Prayer is our answer and response.

When you have a need, talk to God in prayer. When you think you don't have a need, talk to God in prayer. When you don't know what else to do, take a moment for prayer. It is as simple as surrendering everything for that special moment.

SPIDERWEBS

ONE MORNING I PARKED IN our church lot and headed into the sanctuary for worship. As I walked by our beautiful garden, I felt a spiderweb pull across my face and hair. My reaction was the same as anyone's would be. I reached up and tried to pull it off my face right away. (Yuck!)

Those webs were so difficult to see and so sticky! No matter what I did, it felt as if it still in my hair. (You know that feeling, right?) Into the restroom I went to get a towel and water and wiped off my face and hair. I thought it was gone, but five minutes later, I felt another little piece on my ear. That, too, was removed. It was gone. Maybe. Or was it?

For the next half hour, I imagined I still felt it in my hair. I wasn't worried of a spider attack but the feel of a web that wouldn't go away. You know what that is like as you have walked through similar webs in your garden or out in the woods. It is more of an inconvenience but not a feeling any of us enjoy. Maybe there is a fear that there may have been a little spider attached that may still be wandering in my hair! Right? Spiderwebs are sticky, and sometimes even when they are taken away, we still feel as if they aren't.

This has caused me to think about other moments in my life when missteps become like spiderwebs that trap and tangle others without them even knowing what is coming. How often has a casual comment or gossip been repeated, and someone else is hurt by what you have never intended them to hear or feels a pain that you have inadvertently caused? That is no different from a sticky web that isn't seen yet suddenly is there. Each of us has been victimized as well by the anger or selfishness of others, and we know something is going on as we can feel it, but we just can't see it or know for sure.

My first year in college, three of us from my home church were invited to breakfast every Saturday by our residence counselor. The other two were best friends and roommates, but we all knew one another from church. I found out one of them was expelled from school for violating a rule about not having girls in the dorm. His roommate had reported him (for some reason) and caused his buddy to be kicked out of school. As they had been best friends, he couldn't let anyone know. Because of our Saturday breakfasts, everyone assumed I was the culprit. His roommate didn't want anyone to know it was him for fear of losing his friends.

So I was thrown under the bus or tangled in a web woven by others and didn't even know it. For most of the year, many either avoided me or made weird comments that just didn't make sense. I had no clue that I was assumed to be the snitch. I was caught in a web but didn't even know it until one day the roommate finally was able to admit to his friend that he, and not I, was the one who got him expelled from school. And the web was removed.

As for me, a sticky web isn't going to lead to death by a spider, but it certainly is a nuisance and causes discomfort. My first reaction is always to get if off me! But what an image that is of what we call sin. Sin is the opposite of loving God and neighbor. It is about selfishness, jealousy, covetousness, deception, anger, and fear and is the dark side of our nature, which does not reflect the light of God's love. Sin definitely leaves traces or weaves traps that are sometimes intentional and sometimes not. It surprises us and is difficult to get away from.

We are so used to the story of Adam and Eve and the deception of a serpent, but maybe for us the spiderweb is a more understandable expression of the surprise and trap of sin. It is difficult to see it coming, and it is hard to get rid of when we experience its nature. And then it is too late.

What a wonderful image to remind us of the holding power of sin and the reality of how difficult it is to get it off us! At the same time, such an awareness may cause us to consider the webs we often weave and the discomfort they cause for others. But the bottom line is the good news that wherever and whenever we feel trapped by the discomfort of a broken world, God promises to remove what we cannot and forgives what isn't even deserved.

EMPTY NEST

THE ADVENTURE BEGAN EARLIER THIS summer when robins started building a nest on top of my garage door opener. This wouldn't do! I didn't want bird droppings all over my car or robin parents chasing me every time I parked in the garage. The grass and straw for the nest was falling into the chain drive of the opener and would clog it for sure. The nest wasn't finished, so I didn't feel guilty saying "no room here!" and carrying it outside.

A week later a new nest appeared in a hanging basket on my porch by the front door. We always came in through the garage, so that seemed a fair compromise. Over the next two months we watched through the glass on the side of the door as eggs were laid, chicks were hatched, parents came back and forth to feed them, and little robins grew up.

Now the nest is empty, and my routine will never be the same. I've gotten used to a daily picture of the progress and now can only wonder how things will turn out for those fledging robins.

We have all had to deal with empty nests. The home we prepare and live in for any length of time is empty when a divorce happens, a spouse dies, or children grow up and move away. *Empty nester* has become a cultural label that many affix to their situation and daily must contend with. I remember when my first child was born, and in what seemed like such a short time, all four grew up, went to college, and moved away. I have the same options as all of you in similar empty nest living—lament the past or celebrate and move on.

As I reflected on the progression that has led to an empty bird's nest,

I was reminded of a young couple seeking a place for a baby to be born. There was no room in the inn, so they moved out to stay with the animals and had a manger for a bed. They moved on and found new places to live, but I wonder how Mary remembered the manger full of straw that looked so much like a nest. When Jesus left home, the image of that beginning must have caused her to wonder how time had moved so quickly and how her little baby had become a man on a mission. Depression and regret could have kept her locked on the image of that bed of hay where the miracle of life began, but we know something else happened. She celebrated the miracle in her life and became a follower and was led with many others to see what he would become and how he would give meaning to that empty nest.

That journey led her to a cross and a tomb where her fully grown baby was laid to rest. How could she not remember when he was a baby in a manger and now had to accept that his mature body was laid to rest in a new nest called a tomb? A parent is never supposed to see the death of their child, but in that surrender, she had to wonder and reflect on the beginnings in that nest of a manger so many years earlier. And yet just as my robin chicks suddenly left their nest, so Jesus, in the greatest story of all time, escaped the tomb. That nest was empty, and what great joy it brought to Mother Mary and to all of us. God's love does that.

The empty tomb trumps every empty nest, for the miracle of life has its cycles and seasons and moves with the patterns intended by God from the beginning. And to remedy our pain and confusion when our nests turn up empty, God has left the comfort of heaven to embrace a Bethlehem manger and a garden tomb. And then both have been left empty. But there can be not one moment of grief at such changes. The life that has begun in a manger and been filled full in an empty tomb is the gift God has shared with you, with me, and with the entire world.

"The tomb is empty!" was the most powerful message ever shared. Tears turned to smiles, and grief turned to joy, and no life has ever been the same again. We are never alone, and there is no emptiness in our living that has not already been filled full by the love of a God of grace.

One morning I noticed the robin nest was empty, and I was disappointed for not being able to watch what would come next. But the point is there is a next because the nest is empty! Whether I see it or not isn't important because the lives that have hatched in that nest are not about me. And as Jesus reminded an audience one day about God's care for the birds of the air and the lilies of the fields, I must celebrate the miracle of life and the seasons of creation by a loving God.

None of us like to look at empty nests, for they remind us of what has changed and will never be the same. But the empty nest of a garden tomb on Easter proclaims that we will never be the same either, and that neither life nor death nor anything else in all creation can ever separate us from one another or the love of a God who has touched our lives.

How we look at empty nests through the lens of faith certainly changes their meaning and the power of their image. Every empty nest can be full of hope and peace because that is where life has begun. For us, it is always about a God whose love is so immense that he has birthed what we call Easter.

HOME

WE RESCUED A BEAGLE THAT lived his first three years in a cage. He was used for animal research as many beagles are. The local SPCA had a program called Cages to Carefree, which took research dogs and found them real homes. We had had our little guy for a couple of weeks now, and I realized last night this was the first time in his young life that he had a home. I told him that but don't know if he understood or not. I guess we'd have to show him what that meant!

But what does *home* really mean? Growing up in a military family meant we moved often. My home was in Japan, then Kansas, then Washington, DC, and Alabama, and Virginia. We moved often! Every place we lived in was home but only for a little while. In a sense, we were homeless but always had what we called a home. We traveled to new places, had new adventures, and assumed everyone lived that way because that was all we knew. We lived in my first congregation longer than I had lived anywhere in my life. It became a real home! Now Michigan had become home. I guess it takes more than a house or location to make a home.

How can a four-letter word have so many meanings? It's a home run! There is no place like home! She is homeless. Come home to Mama! Home away from home. A home for orphans. A home page on a website. My hometown. ET phone home! I also know people who live in one community but have another cabin, cottage, or house in another community as well. What does *home* mean, and how can one word mean so many different things?

Most assume that a home is where life is centered and involves familiarity, comfort, safety, and hopefully peace. Where is home for you, and what does it take for a place to become your home? I think it is one of those words difficult to explain, but we know it when we see it and relax when we feel it. Are you comfortable in your home, or are you still waiting to feel at home?

A familiar hymn says, "I'm but a stranger here. Heaven is my home," which adds an entirely different feel to the conversation. Some criticize people of faith for being unrealistic about the idea of heaven and insist this present life is all there is. Such an outlook brings tension, frustration, and fear anytime there is a loss of home or an inability to feel at home. I think the lack of understanding of our true home makes it increasingly difficult for many around us to have peace, comfort, and joy, no matter where they live.

A Christmas hymn has the words *from heaven above to earth I come.* That text signals something significant in our understanding of a real home. Jesus has left his heavenly home so that we will find us a home with him now and forever. When we feel the loving embrace of God, we are literally at home wherever we are. That is the miracle he has brought so that no matter what we have or lose, where we find shelter or a place to sleep, we are safely in the arms of a heavenly parent who daily says, "Welcome home!"

I have mentioned the SPCA program that frees animals from cages and brings them into the care and keeping of a forever home. They caution that anyone adopting such animals will need much more love, care, and patience as these animals have never had a real home. *Patience* is the operative word!

That has helped me understand something else. What a wonderful illustration of what God has done in adopting us! We are caged by this world. We are probed and pushed and tempted by forces often beyond our control. But God's love has come to rescue us and bring us into a loving companionship based solely on grace. We don't deserve it, but God's love can't resist bringing us into a forever home with him.

Our beagle, whom we have named Bosco, hasn't done anything to deserve adoption but now will learn what it means to be fed and cuddled and housed in a safe place where there is freedom to make mistakes while surrounded by lives that will keep him safe. It is scary to bring a dog into our home when we aren't certain what he has been through, but God does that for us perfectly as he loves us despite who we are or what we have or haven't done. That is grace! That is my understanding of what home should be.

The good news of Christmas is that God has chosen to make his home with us. That is even more interesting as God has given up everything to live with us so that we will know what love and life really mean. Adoption, any adoption, is the most complete gift of earthly grace that I can think of. And the reality that God has adopted us means that our hearts have been changed by his love, and we are always home because he is always with us. With that comes peace, for we have a forever home.

VACATIONS

FACEBOOK IS THE NEW PLACE where everyone posts highlights of their vacations, whether to the Badlands, Ozarks, Alaska, Yellowstone, or somewhere else. When vacations are as expected (or even better), we feel the price paid and energy expended are more than worth it. On the other hand, when a vacation is a bust, there is often a disappointment, feeling time and money was wasted. *Vacation* comes from a Latin word meaning an exemption or freedom from obligations, burdens, or labor. It is all about relaxing, resting, and being unworried, and yet that is not often the case when we take a vacation.

We have had incredible vacations and some so disappointing that they are embarrassing to discuss. Yet often, it is in those times when nothing has gone right that we have grown to appreciate even more the gift such a time really is. As we consider the real purpose of vacation, we may begin to see how some of our worst vacations have become more memorable than those that are picture perfect.

For instance, a vacation with our kids in Cape Cod in late March was a bust as weather was terrible, and nothing was open. But we spent time together playing cards and talking and figuring out together how best to enjoy one another when there was little to see or do outside. A trip to North Carolina for a family reunion was sidetracked by a rental home that was not even close to what had been described, and terrible weather limited much of what we hoped to do. Yet all our kids and grandkids were under one roof at the same time, which didn't happen often.

When our children were young, we took a dream vacation that included my brother and his wife. After much research and planning, we settled on a lake cottage in Maine, which became a disaster. We prepared for a rustic cabin, like we had seen in movies, with beautiful sunsets, fantastic fishing, and no mosquitoes, only to be greeted with a cabin with only one light, one bedroom, and a shower and toilet in the kitchen. (Oh yeah, giant mosquitoes swarmed and were not held at bay by old and tattered screens.) Yet we'd still talk about those trips today as there was always something good that came out of disappointment. We plan vacations with the idea of a freedom from normal obligations, burdens, or labor. Sometimes it is, and sometimes it isn't, but always it is time that is different.

Roxanne and I just had a minivacation that unexpectedly became something else. Our accommodations and destination were not what we hoped for, yet we found a way to have the unburdening of work and responsibilities in a different way and place than we had planned. Our choice was to suffer, complain, or regroup. Disappointment turned into the relaxation we needed in a different way than first planned. Fortunately (this time), I learned to allow reality to be tempered by a greater reality. I am still learning, but this was one time I did better than usual.

In one of his letters, Saint Paul had an interesting take on such moments as he explained how Christ's grace enables a new approach to earthly disappointments and struggles. He believed that suffering leads to endurance, which builds character, which results in hope. His conviction was that hope in God will never disappoint and will keep us strong no matter what.

What we do with the bad, unexpected, or embarrassing uncovers the reality and basis for who and whose we really are. Whether a vacation gone sour, a world full of confusion and fear, or any other part of a broken creation, without Christ we will be left to ourselves, which won't leave us much to work with. But keeping our eyes focused on God's love and promises first allows us to approach disappointments and often find a silver lining. Remembering what Jesus has done with hostility, misunderstanding, betrayal, painful surprises of a broken world, and even his own death changes who we are and how we live. It really can!

My dad was sent into the Korean War and missed the birth of his first son, yet our relationship was unique because of that beginning and the greater appreciation of our love for each other that would never be taken for granted. A young mom I was well acquainted with faced her untimely death by sharing her love and faith in a unique act of servant love to prepare her husband and young children with confidence, hope, and strength as her parting gifts. This was what Paul was writing about!

Even difficult vacations and painful realities of life can become more than first offered when touched by the healing love of Christ. Our perspective changes when we remember whose we are. In a sense, every day is a vacation as the obligations, burdens, and disappointments of daily loving are lifted by the love of what Jesus has done for us. It is like the rainbow that always comes with the storm.

LETTING GO

MY YOUNGEST CHILD IS NO longer a child. She has grown up, has a real job, and is living in a big city. All my children have followed similar paths away from childhood, but with the last comes a realization that I will not ever experience this transition again. In some ways, that is good; for other reasons, it is difficult. Over the years I have learned (too slowly) that there are many things beyond my control and many of my frustrations have come from trying to hang on to or attempt to change people and situations that are not mine to own.

The first congregation I served was a wonderful place, and we were happy there, but I had become so much a part of every life that I often forgot those lives were not mine but of others. My role was not to protect, fix, and heal everyone else but to share good news, reach out with love, and allow those lives to be. I had to know when and how to get out of the way.

It took time to learn those lives were not mine. It was not for me to feel guilt for mistakes they made, just as it was not proper for me to accept credit for the wonderful gifts they were in their daily lives. Sometimes I forgot that as I cared and worried too much. I wanted to be the first to offer comfort. I felt guilty if I didn't feel I was making a difference. It bothered me when I felt I hadn't worked hard enough to bring peace into conflict or a solution to dissension.

When I left that congregation, I did so not because I wanted to but because I knew I had to. We had made incredible gains in terms of our mission and the feel and flow of congregational life, but it could not always be dependent on me. I needed to learn when it was time to let go and let birds fly on their own. The good people of my first parish taught me how to do that, and in their allowing my family to move on when we felt it was time to do so, I learned about keeping God first and trusting in him more than myself.

As parents, our most difficult moment is when it is no longer appropriate for us to make decisions and take care of all the ins and outs of our children's lives. They are still our children. We continue to be their parents. But as they become adults, our role as parent becomes more of an observer who will always be available when called on but no longer responsible for many of the decisions that we have taken care of for so long.

I did that more successfully with my older children as there was enough to keep me busy with whatever birds were still in the nest. Now that the nest is empty, I need to change hats and not feel guilty or confused about my new role. It is what it is, and I must accept that, just as all of you should.

When my daughter moved into the big city, I worried about the traffic, the problems that could occur, the location and size of her small apartment, her need to find local doctors and dentists. I wanted to keep a hand on her shoulder and felt so protective that I was forgetting to accept the joy and confidence she already had as she was flying on her own and celebrating the successes of her transition. Our goal as parents is to create independent young adults. And when that time comes, it is as it should be.

As I look back, I remember how small our first apartment was. I remember how little money we had. We raised children with no family nearby and dealt with accidents, illness, someone breaking into our home, flooded basements, and never having enough money to be able to save any for a rainy day. But we were happy, our home was full of love, and we celebrated our faith in many ways.

Parenting never ends, but it changes. We all feel guilt for things we wish we had done differently but forget we always have done the best we can. Where we have come up short, God's grace offers the forgiveness we need to accept and allow us the peace that it brings. Where we have been successful, we need to give God the thanks for whatever small role we may have played and let it go at that. Faith is all about letting go, trusting God, and living for today rather than worrying about yesterday or tomorrow.

I am not alone in such a wrestling match. And this is about more than parenting. Our ministry staff has spent countless hours and conversations wrestling with what we need to do in an ever-changing culture with all the realities brought by a pandemic, ever more complicated schedules of our families, and changes in habits and priorities. Ultimately, the answer is the same in how I do ministry as how I must be a parent. I can love, I can support, I can share good news, and then I have to get out of the way.

Ministry, like parenting, is not successful because of me but despite me. Any disappointments are similarly moments of learning, seeking forgiveness and guidance, and then moving on. For each of you, it is the same whether at work, in marriage, in parenting, or in relating to your congregation. If priorities are as they should be, with loving faith coloring our daily responsibilities and actions, we are on the right path. And guilt, fear, worry, or the need to control what we cannot have a hold over needs to be taken off the table.

I am praying that I can learn to do all this more easily, and my youngest daughter's transition to adulthood is another chance for me to learn to trust God, to give up control that is not mine to assume, and to live with the love, joy, and peace that are the assurances of faith and the gifts that do change life! Maybe the best way to define faith is to see it as the gift that allows us to let go.

FRIENDS

I AM HAVING A PROBLEM with Bosco, our new beagle. And I don't understand why. Or maybe it is better to say he is having a problem with me.

He spent his first three years in a cage in a research facility, as many beagles do. We knew he might have some idiosyncrasies, and it would take a while for him to learn how to be a real dog. He still scares easily and is even afraid of the sliding glass door on the deck or any sudden moves or loud noises. I was certain the attention and warmth that we shared would be enough to change him quickly. My expectation was he would be so glad to have freedom and warmth and a new home that he would write thank-you notes on Post-its that I would find when I came home each day. But it hadn't quite been that easy.

Actually, he is great with Roxanne and spends much of his time snuggling next to wherever she sits (when she actually slows down enough to sit). It is embarrassing to admit, but there are times he acts as if he is scared of me, and that bothers me to no end. He is a cute little guy, and I walk him a couple of miles every morning and again in the afternoon or evening. He knows who I am (I think), but sometimes when I walk into the room, he runs to another place in the house. To be honest, it bothers me, for there is no reason for him to be afraid. Sometimes I can sit with him and scratch his ears, and other times, especially if I move too quickly, he is gone in a flash. I don't get it. Maybe I remind him of someone in the lab where he has lived, or it is the timbre of my voice. (I don't think my breath is worse than his, so it can't be that!) Anyway, he is a project as I want him to know I am his friend and not to be feared.

This reminds me of times I want to be friends with others, but they really aren't interested in me. It bothered me then, as it does now, when someone who has been a friend in the past no longer is, and I don't understand why. All of us have such moments when we lose a friend or can't make one, and it just doesn't make sense. All of us want to know we are important to others. All of us need attention, conversation, and friends. Why is it so difficult sometimes, and what do we need to do when things just aren't going the way we want?

On the other hand, there are people who cross our path and desire to be friends with us, but we aren't that interested in them for one reason or another. We know how to avoid those we don't like or whom we really can't see being with frequently, but we often don't take time to think about how our rejections can make them feel. It really is a delicate balancing act we live with every day. We want friends but wish to be able to completely control such endeavors. We don't want to feel pressured to be friends with others who might have interests or plans different from ours. As Christians we are motivated by our desire to be loving and caring, yet sometimes others don't understand the difference between being friendly and being friends. At the same time, others might have similar feelings about us, and we don't understand where they are coming from.

With Bosco the beagle, it is a much simpler dance. I know that the harder I try, the more I will intimidate him. And I know I cannot take it personally, for there is just something in his conditioning or background that makes him act the way he does. And I cannot resent my wife, whom he clings to like a piece of lint on a sweater. In time, we will find our balance, and I am confident he will gradually lose whatever fearfulness he has come to us with. It takes time, and it will be whatever time it takes. He and I will just have to wait each other out, be patient, and find our way. Acceptance is more important than control.

In all this, there are lessons greater than just me and a dog. Life is never as clean and perfect as we want, especially when other lives are involved. Sometimes we find friends in the most unexpected ways. Sometimes friends will cease to be so, and we may never know why. Sometimes we will wander away from others without even being aware we have done so or how our absence may confuse or hurt them. Life is full of surprises and confusing moments, and sometimes the worst thing we can do is make it personal. We simply need to allow time and patience work their magic (like I am committed to with Bosco the beagle). He doesn't have a clue how his distancing has affected me, but it is not his fault, and it is better for me not to assume any motives on this part other than the reality of what I see.

As I wrestle with this issue, I have come to see that, as with so many moments in life, when I slow down, I can figure out what really is bothering me. In this situation with the beagle, his distancing simply raises the hurts that I feel anytime someone else has disappointed or hurt me. I cannot put that burden on him. And in knowing that he is simply reacting to something in his past, I cannot assume his actions are directed against me, which they likely are not.

That helps me be more careful with how I treat others and also in making assumptions about how they treat me. This is not rocket science, but it is just as important. Love and care take patience, persistence, and humility. What we cannot control we should not resent, and what we cannot heal on our own we need to be willing to ask for God's help in moving us forward. I appreciate your patience in allowing me to wander and wonder, and I hope that some of this may prove helpful in some small way for you as well. God's love is greater than our weakness and emptiness. We always have a friend in that relationship, and its fullness changes how we treat and respect each other as we learn to slow down, not take everything personally, and live with humility and love.

WAITING

MOST OF US DON'T WAIT easily or well and are tired of awaiting so many things that we don't want to even think about waiting for anything else. Advent is a season of waiting, and the new church year begins with the theme of waiting. On Christmas this wait will end. This can be a healthy time for spiritual growth as we wait for Jesus to come rather than for everything we are tired of lying in wait for.

Waiting is not my strong suit. One afternoon my difficulty with waiting was given a trial. I was ready for an afternoon of chores after a few days away for a family Thanksgiving in Saint Louis. Roxanne had things to do as well, and we both headed out to the garage. That was where we encountered the problem. Her car was locked, and her key fob wouldn't open the car. So either the fob needed batteries or the car battery was dead. I checked the batteries for the key fob, and they were fine. Uh-oh! Now we were in serious territory as it meant the car battery was dead. I called AAA for a jump start and was told it would be a couple of hours. The waiting began. So I watched some football. Roxanne got busy in the basement with sorting, packing, and getting other stuff done.

The car was in the garage, and it was going to be tough to get jumper cables to the battery. The car was locked with no way to open it. There was a little key in the fob for such emergencies, but it wouldn't open the lock. Now what? More waiting. I watched football and waited for a truck to arrive to help. Finally, I tried again, got the car unlocked, and opened the hood. The waiting continued. And I watched more football. And Rox wrapped gifts.

Five hours later and no help! I made several more calls to AAA and was given different stories each time. Nine hours into the wait, I finally called a local tow company. Soon a truck arrived and got the car running. We drove it to our service facility so a new battery could be installed that day. That wait was over. I did fairly well but wasted most of a day and night doing nothing but waiting.

All of you have had similar waits—for a baby to arrive, guests to leave, enough money to buy a home or car, an illness to be healed, or grief to subside. How we wait is probably more important than what we are waiting for, as each time it is because there is something we cannot control or make happen until it arrives or happens. My waiting is often colored with paralyzing frustration, worry, and anxiety when something is needed that I cannot control. Waiting is never easy, which is why how we do it is so important.

One day I had things I wanted to do but couldn't as I waited. There were other things I could have accomplished had I quit waiting for the phone to ring or a truck to show up. My wait could have been productive like my wife's, but I was waiting in the wrong way, and those nine hours of me sitting would never exist again. It was not productive waiting, and I don't feel good about that today.

That is a reminder for me that anytime I need to wait, I have choices about how. Advent reminds us of how God waited until the time was right to embark on a new way of revealing his love and sharing his gifts. But that was nothing new. From the beginning God had waited for his children to be faithful, loving, and committed to celebrating the gifts of creation in healthy and productive ways. When that didn't happen, God didn't just sit around watching the angels play flag football but kept engaging his love in creative and new ways.

Through miraculous rescue efforts, the messengers called prophets, and the lives of many faithful people, God has continued to share his message of forgiving love and servant surrender throughout time. He has shared wonderful parents and family and friends whose loving lives have been wonderful examples of how God doesn't just sit back but finds ways to touch us! And in the most perfect way, he has revealed the same gifts in a baby in a manger. So you see, there are different ways to wait. Guided by the example and love of God, we discover patience is not simply a virtue but also a trust in the gift of God, who is so active and engaged in every part of our living.

Sometimes we have to wait. Sometimes we choose to wait. Advent is one of those once-a-year reminders of the fact that we are never waiting alone and can choose to complain about waiting or find new ways to be gifts to ourselves and others as we wait in more loving and faithful ways.

When my eyes are open to what is going on around me rather than simply on my waiting, what results is more active and productive than just sitting and waiting for a phone to ring, a baby to be born, or a miracle to be revealed. Allow Advent to be patient, productive, and full of anticipation of the joy that this wait always brings. Focus on the real prize.

Advent is a countdown to Christmas. It is also a pattern to help remember how to live each and every day. Advent doesn't have to be wasteful waiting, as mine has been yesterday, but full of forgiving, serving, engaging, and joyful waiting (which, after all, is what all living really can be).

Often, we will need to wait. What is most important is how we wait.

GIFT GIVING

EVERY YEAR, SOON AFTER THE return to school, we are inundated with ads getting us ready for our annual and intense Christmas shopping. The pressure to shop early and often reminds me of how my brother and I shopped for Christmas as kids. We saved our allowances over the year (which didn't amount to very much) and usually were willing to spend about $5 or so on each other for Christmas. (My sisters were not on our list as they were younger and only sisters.) Don and I were the eldest, and our sophisticated approach to gifts for each other ensured we would both get at least one gift we really wanted. That guaranteed Christmas would always be at least partly successful.

Here is how our gift scam worked. We agreed on how much we could spend. A few Saturdays before Christmas, Dad and Mom took us to the store on the army post called the PX (which was a store like Meijer—one-stop shopping). We would head to the toy department and spend at least thirty minutes looking at which plastic models were available in our price range. We favored airplanes and ships from Revell. Once we had pointed out one or two favorites to the other, we took turns leaving the department so the other could buy the right gift, which would be welcomed with gusto and surprise when opened on Christmas Day. We thought it an extremely clever way to approach gifts.

This brings back wonderful memories, especially as I think about our passion for building models (that wound up being broken every time we moved). It reminds me of how much effort we put into making certain we get exactly what we want. (Christmas is often more about want

93

than need, right?) As I reflect on the internet pressure to buy quickly (as supplies are limited) or the guilt inflicted if we fear disappointing someone, I am embarrassed at how we easily miss the point of the word *gift* in the first place.

For gifts should be planned and motivated by the giver rather than be a demand or expectation of the receiver. The best gifts are those filled with passion, joy, or thanksgiving rather than obligatory gestures to maintain relationships or preventing feelings of guilt later on if we don't meet the expectations of others or the pressure of advertisers.

I can only guess at what my grandparents and previous generations would think if they saw the ever-expanding lists for baby and bridal showers and other gift giving. It is certainly better to give a gift you know someone will appreciate (like my brother and I were so good at doing). Yet when that is the preoccupation, it puts the receiver in control rather than the gift giver, which begs the question of whether *gift* is even the right word. It is worth a little time to consider what the word *gift* means to us and how that might help us as we give and receive.

A *gift* is defined as a voluntary transfer of something with no expectation of payment in return. Such a meaning makes it very one sided. If someone asks or expects, then it isn't a gift. (My brother and I did know that but were using the legal technicalities of grade school to assist our selfish tendencies!) At the same time, whether or not one appreciates what they receive should not diminish the reality of whether it is a gift. Too easily the receiver can control gift giving more than the gift giver, as two brothers did once upon a time. (But don't blame him as I am the one who developed the idea in the first place!)

That puts a new spin on gifts in this season, where gift giving is so much a part of our culture, tradition, and economy. There is a reason for this season. Actually, there are many reasons. Whichever reason is most important will have an impact on the definition of *gift*, both on how we give and how we receive.

For Christians, this is a season to celebrate the birth of the Messiah. A baby in a manger was not a desired or expected gift. The world wanted something more powerful, more glamorous, as in a king who would ensure his followers had everything they wanted or needed. Instead, God chose a baby who would live only to surrender his life out of love for you and me.

Christmas is our annual moment to celebrate the greatest gift ever. One way to celebrate is by responding with gifts. That is, well, a special part of our joy. Since that is our tradition, it makes sense to remember why we give and how we receive. It is a season of gifts for reasons such as joy, hope, and peace!

When Jesus was born, many said either, "Ho hum," or "Not what we hoped for." We are blessed today to realize God has given more than what has been expected or deserved. Our lives will never be the same due to such a gift. In response, we share our joy in the shape of gifts. And whatever we receive makes more of an impact when we consider the motivation of the giving rather than the price or color of the gift.

Years ago I never appreciated the white handkerchiefs Grandma sent every year. But now I would give anything to hug Grandma again rather than complain about the only gift she could afford. In our gift giving and receiving, we have an opportunity to remember what undeserved love means. As we respond to a baby in a manger we haven't asked for but has changed us forever, we learn from the best gift of all.

ROUGH SLEDDING

MY BROTHER AND I HAD one sled we had to take turns on. It was a Flexible Flyer, the Cadillac of sleds! They still make them but at a price quite a bit more than what I know ours cost. We loved that sled and used wax paper to wipe the steel runners to make it even faster. (I do not know if it made a difference or not, but we were sure it did!)

We had a great steep sledding hill. When the snow was just right, it felt like we were flying. The only problem was it had no cushioning or way to absorb shocks along the way. As fast and smoothly as the sled performed, when the hill began to ice up, we would feel every bump, and the sledding became increasingly rough. As a bonus, hidden rocks and sticks under the snow created bumps we could not have seen and thumps we certainly felt. The longer we sledded, the more aches we would come home with. But we always went back for more.

It was frustrating when sledding became rough as that caused many tumbles and spills as well as the inevitable bruises we would come home with. The smiles and smooth sledding we saw on the TV commercials were not always what we were privileged to experience. Don't get me wrong, we sledded anyway, but sometimes we came home with bumps and scrapes we hadn't planned on.

We all know firsthand what difficult times feel like. The image of smooth versus rough sledding is one we know all too well. A perfect vacation becomes a series of unplanned surprises that makes one wonder whether it should have been undertaken at all. The perfect job is lost, a great relationship suddenly struggles, and inevitably, we have more aches and pains after sixty than at twenty. We plan for smooth sledding but are disappointed and traumatized when what should have been pleasant becomes a time in which we find ourselves battered and bruised. That is not always the case as many moments in life are perfect, wonderful, and better than we have hoped. But when the sledding gets rough, we find ourselves wondering, complaining, and looking for help.

Remember a day when Jesus took the guys on a boat ride on the lake that they had fished all their lives and knew so well? Out of the blue, a storm came up that was so severe they were certain they would die. Even though they had seen his miraculous deeds and felt his compassionate love, they feared for their lives and were amazed that he seemed to sleep through the roughest boat ride they could remember. Smooth sailing they could handle, but rough sledding always got their attention and caused them to forget what was more important than their fear and panic. (Sounds familiar? Of course, it does!)

Jesus calmed the storm and stilled the waters. He took the rough edges off the lake and eased the fears of his disciples and friends. It only took a word, and the lake was smooth as glass, and the sun chased away the clouds of that storm. It reminds us of creation, where a mere word from God brought everything into existence. Hard to imagine, but faith calls us to believe. It only takes a word from God, and the world stands still. And when the sledding gets rough, it is that word we need to remember more than the bumps that are causing us to bruise.

In that same spirit, remember when the prophet Isaiah made a promise that God would come charging out of the forsakenness of the desert and create an avenue for God to change our lives? He said valleys and mountains would become the same level highway. He promised the journey would be a smooth and easy one to embrace. He was speaking to exiles waiting to return home and promised that in this trip out of exile, which God had planned for them, they would see his glory. Every Advent, as we near Christmas, we hear those same words.

On a day after a terrible storm, the disciples certainly saw the glory of the Lord revealed after his word stilled a storm and calmed the sea. After that horrendous sight of their Master hanging from a cross on Calvary, they witnessed the brightest sunrise ever when the stone was rolled away from the tomb. And that is the good news we must never forget. Our loving God is daily by our side, seeking to heal us from rough sledding and take the bruises and fears of a broken world out of sight and out of mind. It is healing and peace he brings for all those moments when we are fearful that the sled has gotten out of control or is bumping and bouncing and we just can't seem to find any smooth patches on which to smoothly slide.

God never promises life will be perfect, sledding will always be smooth, or the lake will always be calm. But he does promise his love will be with us, and he will do for us what we need and care for us more than we deserve. That is the power of his love and the truth of his promise. And never forget: even when the clouds are darkest and the gloom deepest, the sun still shines behind those clouds and, when the storm is over, will shine as brightly as it has done before the storm. Just like God's love, it is there even when clouds seek to hide it!

It only took a word for God to create galaxies and butterflies. It only took a word for a storm to cease so the troubled would remember who they were with. And that same word breaks into each and every one of our lives. *Peace! Be still! I am with you and will never let you go.* In other words, there is smoother sledding ahead!

GRACE

A NEW MINISTRY THE COVID-19 pandemic brought into being was the Facebook messages I shared twice weekly with our congregation. One morning I was stumped and having great difficulty coming up with something fresh and new. I racked my brain, said a few prayers, and tried to think of any events in recent days. Yet no matter what I did, I had nothing. It was a frustrating moment, to say the least.

I read through old articles I had written, looked for old sermon illustrations that maybe had never seen the light of day, and just wandered through computer files, trying to generate an idea that would be worthwhile for others. In doing so, I ran across a sermon I had written almost twenty years ago for my eldest son's wedding. For reasons I would explain, I had never looked at that sermon again as it was terrible. I am not certain how or why I found it this morning, but I did.

Two weeks before his wedding, our eldest daughter had suddenly died. We buried her a week before my son was to be married. The last thing I had energy or creative juices for was a wedding. We were trapped between the grief of loss and the joy of a marriage. I tried to back out, but he needed me to be with him for the same reasons I really didn't want to have to say anything.

He was trapped in the emotional upheaval of losing his sister and best friend just as he was to begin his new life with his new best friend for life. I had agreed a year earlier to perform his wedding, even though I worried how well I would do as I can get very emotional at such special moments in my children's lives (just as all of you do). So rather than be a spectator,

99

I had agreed to stand with my son and his bride at that most important day. And then events occurred that no one could have imagined possible, as we celebrated a marriage in the Chapel of the Resurrection at Valparaiso University.

I had never looked back at the sermon until I searched through old files. And it would have been best to leave it well enough alone. I read it and could not believe how terrible a message it was. It was a standard wedding sermon but was not any normal wedding due to circumstances beyond our control. The guests were all family and close friends, which meant we all knew what was going on, and no one was going to be very critical of me for such a terrible message.

It was so surreal as we all wanted to be there, yet none of us wanted to be there. We felt guilty about being joyful but would have been more so if we had not celebrated the marriage. To make matters worse, I couldn't and didn't say anything of any help to the moment. Part of my problem was if I had really addressed the grief of that moment, I would have broken down and been incapable of "doing the wedding." I avoided what I was having trouble dealing with solely to be able to get through the moment the best I could. So the sermon was terrible, but we were still able to genuinely celebrate the joy of a marriage.

The reason I share this is for us to remember that sometimes we just don't know what to do or say. We just do the best we can and surrender that effort to God's grace. These past months have been filled with such confusion with nasty political debates, upheavals in our cities, and a pandemic that keeps finding new ways to keep going as we try our best to live as normally as possible while still finding find joy and peace during troubling and painful events.

Daily we feel guilt for joy and successes as others struggle with loss and grief. And there are difficult moments when we honestly resent others for their smiles and ease of living while we stumble with uncertainty and pain. We often cannot come up with the right words or feelings and find that our best efforts are embarrassingly weak (like my sermon at my son's wedding).

Upon reflection, no one likely even listened to my words at the wedding, for all were wrestling with the same issues. No matter how poorly constructed and delivered my meager effort was, the fact that I was standing with my son and his bride and our family and friends was the miracle of that moment. By grace, we did what none of us thought was possible! That alone was a wonderful beginning for my son and his wife, just as it helped all of us move forward.

We were doing the best we could, and God blessed that moment. That is what being people of faith is all about! Being together with genuine efforts at joy and support is a miracle I appreciate better today than I have done then. For people of faith, it is all and always about grace. We do our best and trust God will do the rest. Because of God's love, even our weakest moments are filled with strength beyond what we can muster. Hope and peace are greater than what we deserve.

No matter how poorly you feel you are handling life or how uncertain you are of the best way to proceed, faith daily assures we are never alone. By grace, God will keep us safe and bring peace beyond any human understanding. My efforts on that day have been inconsequential compared with the love of Christ, which has allowed us to be together as one, cognizant of our loss and lifted by the power of faith, hope, and love!

And that, my friends, is the most important message for each of us in every moment of our lives. The grace of God, which fills our lives daily, more than compensates for any weakness. And so it will always, by faith and grace, be! Do your best and be at peace!

LOVE SONGS

THINK ABOUT LOVE SONGS AND why they are so important. Whatever music we have listened to in our teens and twenties will likely be the love songs we remember the best. You can probably get a good clue about anyone's age by asking what their favorite love songs are. My dad likely listened to Peggy Lee or Judy Garland, while Mom probably favored Frank Sinatra or Perry Como. Mine were all from Motown artists. What about you? Love songs are memorable as they speak to the emotions of our heart—and still do!

Every Thursday I'd record a sermon for the radio. One day the text for my sermon was Jesus's prayer at his last meal with the disciples before his crucifixion. Preparing to die, he took time to share his love with a prayer that God would help them through the most difficult and painful moments they would ever face. The entire evening was a love song of sorts, beginning with a meal, then a foot washing, and finally this prayer. When the disciples faced the pain of the cross, his words and actions helped them feel the extent of his love for them. The same holds true for us today.

Considering this prayer as a love song to help disciples, I thought about my children. Because we had faced similar rough moments, we had gotten used to finishing every phone call with the words *I love you*. That was so helpful when, unexpectedly, my eldest daughter died. The last words we shared were *I love you*. There is no doubt God inspired that gift, which carried me through a grief I was not ready for. But what a gift it was! I share this only because I want you to believe God's love is stronger than anything we forget or remember. Now I come to the real point of this meditation.

I offered these same thoughts at the end of my radio sermon with great difficulty as they caused memories to come flooding back. As I walked away from the studio, I apologized to Neil (who did our recording) for getting personal as I never wanted a sermon to sound as if I was talking about me. Neil was gracious in saying he appreciated the connection of life to God's love. I thanked him but still felt that I had gone too far. It was the same for any of us when we'd open such painful moments that always seemed to take another little piece of us away.

I got into my car to leave, and then the phone rang. It was my brother. He called to let me know Dad had just died. We knew this day was near, and he and my sister had driven out from the East Coast to be with Dad. My other sisters and I had called two days earlier saying the day was close. They drove all night just to get there in time, which they did. My first thought was thankfulness they had gotten to be with Dad. Then I remembered more.

Two days earlier, when I left Dad at the nursing home, I kissed him on the forehead and said, "I love you, Dad," as I always did.

Even though he was not speaking much at all in the last months of his life, he said in reply, "Love you!" I am not certain how or why this was the text or the sermon that happened to be up for that week. But it was.

As I cried in the car, I thought about apologizing to Neil, who recorded my sermons, for going off script and getting so personal. Then I remembered his loving words of assurance to me. I really hadn't gone off script after all. In faith, we are always close to God and his love as there are so many ways we are reminded of his lyrics of love. John's Gospel shares Jesus's love song of prayer for his disciples (and us). How can I not remember my own love songs with those who are so important to me? And then I was ready to face another earthly loss and heavenly gain.

Love songs are the only songs that change what we can't and fill what we fear. And please don't think this is about me, for it isn't. For there have been too many other words spoken by me over the years I would rather forget. That is why forgiveness is one of God's most precious gifts! His song of love overrides every loveless word and empty moment of life. When the song is love, we can truly bear one another's burdens and rise above weaknesses and misspoken words. Because of God's love for me, I am forgiven, I am renewed, I am strengthened, and I have a model of how I may seek to live in a new way.

So here is the bottom line: never quit singing the love song that has changed your life. If we can remember popular songs from high school and college years and they still touch a special spot in our hearts, how much more will Jesus's love song to us change our hearts forever and for always?

If you haven't heard his song of love for you in a while, take some time to listen more closely. And if you haven't said "I love you" as much as you may, today is a wonderful time to make certain you do. It is truly easier to say "I love you" than you may imagine. And in time, we get used to saying it often. Life, after all, always should be about love, correct? And there is no love with a stronger melody or memory than God's song of love to us, and those lyrics are easy on our ears and wonderful to share with others.

SEPARATION

MY WIFE WILL TELL YOU I do not do well with separation from loved ones. It is difficult to say goodbye, even when we are not far from one another. I don't know why, but even when I am excited by a journey or a vacation, when the moment comes to leave home, it is the same as when my children return to their homes. My stomach gets nervous, I feel like crying, and a weight seems to hang over me. I do not do well with separations. Maybe it is because of losses in my life or because I have been so blessed with incredible loved ones I truly enjoy being with, but I just know that such moments bring a predictable response.

My parents were more incredible than I realized as a child, and one of their standards for travel would never be forgotten. Before we packed everyone in the station wagon for a summer vacation or a trip to grandparents who lived many states distant, Dad always did the same thing. He made us sit at the dining room table and always said a prayer. He prayed for a safe journey and for God to watch over us while we were away. I guess that was part of my parents' prayers as well when each of us moved out of the house, got married, or moved far away. Dad always did it right!

My aunt Barb loved to end phone calls and letters with a Hebrew word of blessing, *mizpah*. That was her way of saying, "Be at peace, for someone is watching over you." It came from an encounter in Genesis between Abraham and Laban where they built a watchtower that would stand between their two lands. The place was called Mizpah, and Laban prayed that the Lord would always stand between the two of them, even when they were out of each other's sight. My favorite memory of my aunt Barb was always her farewell of mizpah, so full of loving blessing. And it was a reminder there was never a need for goodbye, for we were always tied to each other even when far away.

I was in one of my separation funks as the youngest of my children, and the last to leave home, was moving to the big city of Chicago. I knew she wouldn't be that far away, but she would be out of sight. As college was behind her and with a job in hand, she was ready to spread her wings and fly. And that day, for me, was filled with the tinge of emptiness and sadness I always felt when it was time to let go and the reality of a separation was in the wind. I felt a loss and a sadness that all could understand.

One of my favorite stories from the Bible was the book of Ruth, a powerful story of grace and a hint of an even greater love that would come many years later. Ruth was a foreigner, married to the son of an Israelite mother named Naomi. They lived in Ruth's land of Moab. When Naomi's husband and Ruth's husband both died, Naomi told Ruth she was heading back home to Bethlehem. She wanted to make certain Ruth was not tied down with caring for an old widow.

Ruth's surprising response to Naomi, who had lost everything and had no one to care for her, was simple. She begged her mother-in-law not to send her away and promised that she would go wherever Naomi went and would live with her and love her. She said, "I will be part of your family, I will accept your faith, and where you die, I will die." She said she would not let anything separate them from each other!

What a foreshadowing, in the Old Testament, of the underserved love with which God touches each of us through the gift of Jesus's sacrifice and the presence of his Holy Spirit. No matter where we journey or who journeys away from us, we are never alone. And when we are tied to loved ones in the same way, even when out of sight, we are still together. That is stronger than the losses we feel so deeply or the anxiety that separation brings.

My separation anxiety always calms as I remember my father's example of prayer before such moments and my aunt Barb's trademark line of "mizpah." They continue to bless me with the gift of a powerful presence that changes every empty moment and that a world full of emptiness and distancing will do well to remember or learn from those of us who know the truth. For God is greater than any earthly separation!

"Mizpah! I am with you! Peace!" And there are even more ways to say the same thing and remember the real tie that binds!

SCHOOL BUS

MY DOG WALK IN THE predawn darkness is now complicated by the presence of school buses roaming the neighborhood. As Bosco the beagle has spent his first three years caged in a research facility, he is just learning how to be a real dog with the ins and outs of a big, scary world. His first encounter with the rumbling noise of a bus in the dark, with its abundance of flashing lights, has been a moment of terror for this little beagle. Acclimation is occurring, but that first experience reminds me of another youngster's encounter with a bus years ago.

Our youngest refused for three weeks to get on the bus for kindergarten. She did just fine walking to the stop and waiting with us and other kids and their parents and didn't bolt when the bus came rumbling toward us. But when the others took that first big step (and it was quite a high step) into a dark bus, she froze, tears formed, and she refused to get on. We drove her for several weeks until she was ready to give it a try and found out she could do it after all.

We were so frustrated at her refusal to get on the bus. We didn't know what to do and didn't understand her fears, but obviously she had some. At the time, I didn't even think to get down on my knees and look up at the bus from the same viewpoint as a five-year-old, but that might have helped. For any of us, a first encounter with something unexpected is always a shock. And the fear about whether that bus would even bring her back home had to be something every munchkin dealt with in different ways.

I had a flashback to that moment with the fear our new dog faced. It forced me to consider something I never had before. We are all wired differently, and there are similar experiences we deal with in different ways. I rode a bus in first grade but couldn't remember the first time or whether it was an issue. We had tickets, and my worry about losing a ticket was greater than my concerns about the bus. As the eldest of my siblings, maybe I was afraid to admit fear, which could have made it easier, but there were many other moments that did strike terror into my life, just as when Abby couldn't get on the bus.

Life is full of many surprises we have never faced before. In the Bible, Jacob ran from Esau in fear for his life. Even when he returned, he feared Esau would find a way to get even. Joseph was thrown in a pit by his brothers and sold into slavery. Jesus's disciples got caught in a storm on the lake and just knew they would drown. On the night of his betrayal, Jesus prayed in the garden with such intensity that some said his sweat was tinged with blood. Then there was that thing called a cross! We forget sometimes God's incarnation means Jesus has taken on every emotion that we deal with.

Some assume Jesus shouldn't have been afraid of suffering and death, but the Gospels indicate he has prayed for God to provide another avenue, if possible. But Jesus has stood firm, and we have the benefit of his love for us, which never wavers!

That same night as Jesus anticipated the fear his disciples would face when they heard he had died and later when they would have to face persecution and death for following him, he promised his disciples that God's Holy Spirit would fill them with understanding of all that he had shared. Furthermore, he promised God would gift them in ways the world could not with a presence the world would never understand. He assured them their fear would be replaced with his precious gift of peace.

Such peace may be the most important earthly gift God brings. When we face what we have never encountered or had trouble dealing with before, God promises that if we look to him, there will be peace. That may not decrease fear or pain but will carry us safely to what comes next.

When my mom was a few days from her earthly death, I could sense something had changed in her appearance and energy level. I finally dared to ask how she was feeling. Her answer was simply, "I don't know. I have never done this before." And then I knew what she knew. She was facing something more anxiety ridden than a school bus or a storm, but her faith was helping her face and share it in a peaceful way. And that helped me as well.

She is the one who has always told me, "Remember whose you are." In such remembering comes a calm (called peace) that makes no sense to the world but is a precious gift for people of faith. Peace! As Jesus has said, this is not something the world can give but a gift that comes from the assurance of Christmas and Easter and the acceptance that we are never alone.

My understanding of God's many promises is that anxiety is best replaced with trust that God will grant the peace that is beyond our human understanding. We will all have moments when we walk through the dark, face the unknown, or are caught by painful surprise. But we walk with a new assurance called peace. And that is a wonderful gift to embrace, to be thankful for, and to share with someone else who can use such help!

TWENTY YEARS LATER

IN EVERY GENERATION THERE ARE dramatic moments that become part of our very being. For my grandparents it is moments such as World War I and the Great Depression. For my parents it is Korea and Vietnam. For me it is the assassinations of Kennedy and King, the explosion of the space shuttle *Challenger*, and the destruction brought about by hijacked airliners. There are equally powerful, more personal moments that have the same effect such as births, deaths, and marriages, which all are burned into our memories and influence how we prioritize living.

On September 11, 2001, I was driving to a meeting of pastors just as a news flash on NPR announced a plane had crashed into one of the towers of the World Trade Center in New York City. The first reports were low key as many thought it was a private plane. But twenty-two minutes later, when another hijacked airliner crashed into the building, everyone knew this was more than an accident. Another jet flew into the Pentagon, and one crashed in Pennsylvania. It was becoming apparent that this was a terrorist attack on our nation. How does one know how to react to something that has never been experienced?

I kept moving in and out of my meeting to get new updates on the radio (I didn't have a smartphone yet) and remembered my sister and her husband lived and worked in Washington, DC. My brother-in-law was serving in the Pentagon on active duty. He was working where one of the planes crashed. In such moments we all worry and wonder and aren't sure what to do but always want to do something. I called my sister Becky to see if Tony was OK. She was very upset, saying she didn't know. She couldn't get through to him as all the phone circuits were busy in the city. I told her I would try, just in case. And I got through. I spoke to Tony, who assured me he was OK and asked me to call my sister for him, which I did. Yesterday she thanked me again for that phone call twenty years ago, which eased her concern even as the grieving for lost friends and a terrified nation was beginning.

I hadn't thought about that in a long while, but her call to me spurred that memory. I felt so helpless in that moment as it seemed our world was about to be taken into a terrible place. By calling my sister, which was all I could think to do, I unwittingly was able to actually be of some help. Things didn't always work that way, but this day it did. If I hadn't called her, she still would eventually find out her husband was safe. But a simple call helped her find that out much sooner. Maybe it was not a big deal, but for her in that moment, it was.

I learned an important lesson that day: sometimes we are useful simply by reaching out to others. Especially when we love someone, we should always err on the side of reaching out rather than holding back. My moment of helpfulness on that day paled in comparison to the bravery exhibited by passengers on airliners and firemen who rushed into collapsing buildings. But even a small moment of love is still significant. Don't ever be afraid to risk taking a moment to touch another life. One never knows how that may become more than either has ever bargained for. Even if you aren't certain exactly what to say or do, just take that small step, and you will always be glad you did.

CHIPMUNK

THIS MEMORY IS NOT FOR the faint of heart! This morning I saw
something I had mixed feelings about and wished to share. I was driving
next to a barn on a friend's property. One of their cats, a tawny little
princess of a feline, came trotting down the road, proud as could be, with
a limp chipmunk hanging from its mouth. The cat had done its duty as a
cat and hunter, and the chipmunk definitely got the short end of the deal.
I would love to have had my camera to illustrate my comments, for there
was no way to see certain things and not have a reaction. There was no
moral judgment attached to what the cat did; it was simply being a cat.

This was illustrative of life's reality. Perspective changes depending
on which side of the fence you may be. Whether you are hunted or the
hunter, life is like that. I could not help but smile as I saw how proud a
successful little cat had been. Like a child bringing home a drawing from
kindergarten who couldn't wait for Mom to attach it to the fridge, this cat
was looking for affirmation as soon as it got home. (Certainly, it was more
instinctive than rational thought process, but none of us are immune from
similar instinctive rather than thoughtful moments!)

Then there was a sad feeling for the loss of a life, especially a little
chipmunk. Even though it was a relative of the tribe of squirrels and
chipmunks that savaged my bird feeders, it still was a life created by God
that ended too soon (from the perspective of the chipmunk). And that
caused an inner pain and maybe even a little anger at a cat that was daily
fed all the food it needed yet was genetically wired to grab a chipmunk
that it would only play with and not even eat.

Mixed feelings are an understatement as I've witnessed this scene today, which has caused me to consider similar daily scenes in our living. Nature has a pattern based on instinctual need. For each step on the food chain ladder, there are surprises above and below. In this moment a chipmunk lost, and a cat won, but there could just as easily have been a coyote walking down the path with the cat in its mouth. The side of the fence we stand on or our position in the hierarchy or societal value can change our perspective.

Every day we see headlines about terrible things someone has done and cries for punishment. (And isn't it difficult to resist joining those voices of the crowd?) How often have we reacted with satisfaction as justice is served or with horror as someone escapes punishment they deserve? And how often has our inner voice whispered, *There, but for the grace of God, it could have been me.* For we all have made mistakes of judgment, action, or inaction that usually has no effect on anyone else and maybe has not been noticed at all. However, in a different context or a different culture, we just as easily can be the victim being dragged off for vengeance or punishment.

That may seem an extreme and impossible possibility, but is it really? How often have we said something in the heat of a selfish moment that may have gotten us fired from a job or on the cover of a newspaper as an example of insensitivity or poor common sense? How often have we been tempted to react to a personal slight with harshness but have had the good sense to refrain from what may have escalated into something with no good outcome?

I know how easy it is for me to condemn and criticize others for being hateful, selfish, or angry, while forgetting my own blunders and broken moments. Spending too much time reveling in the imperfections of others keeps us from forgetting the reality of how sin taints us all.

This all started with a happy cat and a disappointed rodent. I am certain the chipmunk's family had a totally different take on the scene than the family and friends of the cat. And should a coyote have found the cat before the cat spotted the squirrel, the family of the cat would have a different reaction as well. It is always about perspective. Life will never be perfect, so why are we so surprised and willing to condemn others who are broken just like you and me?

We are pulled into so many debates and conflicts in politics, at work, among families, and even among strangers when we forget none of us are as blameless as we want others to think and all of us fall short of God's glorious plan. We all will do better to understand the causes of brokenness that get out of control and how God's grace may bring a new gift into the mix. Better it would be for me to respond to such pain and brokenness in a similar fashion as how I want to be treated by God and those who are around me!

Daily God provides glimpses and scenes we cannot ignore and have strong feelings about. Like the voice of prophets, such moments have the potential to resist the urge to react without first considering what it is we are really seeing and respond in the reality of whom God has created us to be. God's gifts of faith, hope, and love are given for a reason and can be utilized more effectively if they are put into play more often.

There are patterns and cycles of life that are often difficult to explain and complicated to respond to perfectly. They are truly embarrassing when we feel as if we are looking in a mirror. A greater fact of life is the love of God, which frees us from our brokenness and calls us to learn to forgive and serve as God has. Paul had it right when he said we all fall short of God's glory. That is something we need to remember more often. And even more important is to remember God's call for us to learn from his example and be a light in a dark world. Keep life in perspective and let us allow the shadow of the cross be more important for us than the darkness of a broken world.

PRAYER

"NOW I LAY ME DOWN to sleep, I pray the Lord my soul to keep." Ever hear or say that? How about "Come, Lord Jesus, be our guest"? When do you pray, and what do you say? Is it a habit, or is it something that happens from time to time?

I could never remember not praying at home! Mom and Dad taught their children to pray. We prayed before and after every meal. I am so glad they did. "O give thanks to the Lord, for he is good!" I just remembered that one too!

Whether a thought or a pattern of words, whether standing or kneeling, whether eyes are closed or open, whether hands are folded or not, there are innumerable postures and patterns associated with prayer. But the purpose rather than the ritual is what is most important. Prayer is a special connection with God.

We should never compare our ability, willingness, or pattern to anyone else, for we are all different. Even thoughts about God or casual comments such as "God, help me!" are prayers. All of us pray; whether as often as we should isn't the issue right now. I will just have you think about prayer. My parents were not Bible-thumping, stiff, or rigid people of faith. They were very intentional but personal and relaxed in how they went about their own patterns of prayer.

What I remember from when the family prayed together at home or in worship continues to be a wonderful gift for all their kids. Our parents helped us understand prayer by how they prayed. They said some prayers over and over again, which helped us learn the basics, such as before and after a meal or when we went to bed. At the time, I just did it. Now I understand what a gift they have given to us without us even realizing it.

One day when Abby was little, she and I were on one of our Friday lunch dates and quietly shared our mealtime prayer before we ate. Later, a lady came over and thanked me for teaching my child to pray. That caught me by surprise, for it was a quiet, private thing for us. It is a reminder that others learn from us, just as I learned from Mom and Dad. We do not pray to be seen, but prayer has side effects we may never imagine.

There is nothing we can tell God he does not already know (even our requests and demands). Nothing can surprise God, so giving God information is not really the purpose of prayer time. Rather, just as in counseling, the act of honestly opening up to God is what helps one admit, rather than hide from, what is so bothersome or burdensome. Prayer allows us to be honest with ourselves about what God already knows. In doing so, we are unloading in the right arena and trusting the right listener. Most importantly, we acknowledge our dependence and trust in God. That is what we call faith!

Everyone has ideas for the type of prayer, the pattern of prayer, and which prayers are appropriate for which times. But if we stick to the basics and remember that prayer is a gift that enables a special connection and communication with God, we can never go wrong. Over time I have grown to learn some of the most important times of prayer are when I say nothing but learn to listen for what God may have to say or remind or reveal. Some of the best prayers are experienced in silence!

Mom always sat us down in the family room before we headed out for a vacation, and Dad would offer a simple prayer asking God to keep us safe. Maybe because his grandparents died in a car crash, that was more on his mind than ours. Unfortunately, I have not always kept that habit in my arsenal, unless a plane ride becomes bumpy or a snowstorm on the interstate becomes blinding. But at least I remember that I can say a prayer, and now that I am thinking about this, I am reminded it is OK to pray more often than I do.

Prayer is not just for when I need something but also helpful in reminding me what is important in my life and the lives around me. In Mom and Dad's later years, they had developed some new patterns of prayer I had not seen when I was young. Maybe it was because they had more quiet time, or more likely, the experiences of life simply had taught them to stick close to God every day. But they added a new prayer to their routine.

After daily morning devotion, they prayed out loud asking God to care for each sibling and spouse, each child and grandchild, every nephew and niece, and other loved ones by name! What a gift of love that is, and it opens to me another reason for prayer. What greater gift can we offer a loved one than to commend them to the care and keeping of a loving God?

We all pray. It is one of the greatest gifts God has shared. That conduit and connection is always open for speaking, for listening, for remembering, and for just being in the presence and shadow of love that surrounds and protects. What a gift prayer can be when as natural as the rhythm of our beating hearts.

UNEXPECTED SMILE

ROXANNE AND I HAD A fantastic trip to Ireland. As I was reviewing some of our many pictures from the trip, I found one that stimulated another memory and made me smile. It was a great memory that was worth spending more time on.

Our trip to Ireland was one in which we did all the driving. It was just the two of us on an adventure. We wanted to visit western Ireland, stay in small towns, and get a feel for the real Ireland. And we are glad that we did. This was our first European vacation, and we decided Ireland was a good place to stick our toe in the water as we could find people who spoke our language and find food that would not be terribly unfamiliar.

My camera is legend among family and friends as is my philosophy. Why take only one picture if you can take twenty? My defense is if I am likely never to cross that path again, I want as many scenes to remember as I can get. In other words, I have taken a lot of pictures. And there is one I am glad I have not missed.

We were in a tiny village on the western coast of the island. We had walked through a linen shop, grabbed a snack in a gas station, and saw an old church. That was about all there was to that town. As usual, I kept stopping to take pictures of signs, buildings, and anything that grabbed my attention. We were just about to cross the road after taking a few pictures of an old church graveyard when I heard a voice (not from the graveyard but the street).

I turned and saw a workman holding a sign that said "stop" on one side and "go" on the other. If any cars showed up, which didn't seem that likely since we had only seen one car in the last ten minutes, he would jump into action. I looked his way as I realized he was talking to me. I hadn't heard what he said at first, so he repeated, "How about taking a picture of me?"

He had a big smile as he asked. I wasn't sure if he was just bored, serious, or poking a little fun at the tourist, but we had already had wonderful moments talking with people we bumped into, so I took his picture (well, actually, several). He laughed and went back to his work of holding a sign. I asked if he wanted me to send him a copy. He laughed and declined but smiled again and thanked me for taking his picture.

As with so many other moments in life, I find that when I slow down and pay attention to what is around me, I am often surprised by how things that seem so normal and simple can have such a powerful impact. We would never see this guy again, but for whatever reason that chance encounter occurred, it had obviously left a memory for me that made me smile every time I thought of it. We found exactly what we hoped for in that trip, and this was just as powerful a moment for me in hindsight as some of the abbeys, castles, and scenery that we saw as well.

We made a brief connection because a guy, who had no need to, stopped what he was doing, smiled, and asked a simple question. I am embarrassed to consider how often I miss a smile, a question, or the reaching out of someone else because I am too busy, too tired, or too selfish to spend time outside my little area of awareness.

Maybe that is why vacations are so important and why I enjoy seeing people and places I would never have seen, rather than doing exactly what I can do at any other time or place. When I break my routine and allow others to break in, that is how strangers (or, once in a while, angels) can touch us with a change that is needed more than we know. It is a reminder too of the power of a smile or a simple request and what happens when I don't look the other way or insist I am too busy to allow an unexpected moment to touch me.

Maybe that guy did the same thing for anyone who walked by with a camera, but I doubt it as there were not too many tourists or tour buses in that little village. It was a smile and a life I would never forget. And what was never planned at the moment was that his smile was one that would now touch you as well. Enjoy the moment!

SURPRISES

WHEN WE TRAVELED TO IRELAND, we prepared for everything we could think of, especially rain. We arranged for a driving tour for just the two of us. We would stay in bed-and-breakfasts and be our own tour guides. We flew into Shannon Airport, landed at six o'clock on a Sunday morning, and picked up our rental car. I knew I would have to drive on the opposite side of the road and hoped I would get used to that quickly. But with all our preparations, there was one reality I hadn't even considered and wasn't prepared for.

The rental cars had standard transmissions, meaning I would have to shift through all the gears (just like the good old days). That was no problem, but my stomach started churning as I wondered if clutch and brake pedals were reversed due to the steering wheel being on the other side of the car. Panic set in. Fortunately, clutch, brake, and accelerator pedals were all in the same place as I learned, but I did have to shift with my left hand rather than my right.

We headed out of the parking lot and immediately encountered a traffic circle! The fact that we had been awake all night and were extremely tired would only make concentration more difficult. *Stay on the wrong side of the road. Shift with the left hand. Go clockwise rather than counterclockwise through the roundabout. Get used to road signs in kilometers.* Luckily, it was early on a Sunday, we were in a small town, and there was no traffic. I went twice around the traffic circle to get a feel for all the new things to remember. And to be honest, I was nervous about having to drive on the real road.

Anytime we turned at an intersection or came out of a roundabout, Roxanne's role was to remind me to get back on the "wrong side of the road." Obviously, we survived! We had worried about the rain but had a week full of sunshine. We worried about getting lost but never did. We had a fantastic experience. Despite all we worried about and planned for, I was caught by surprise. And as I said, we survived driving on the wrong side of the road and shifting with the wrong hand.

Everyone has similar experiences, often much more dramatic and serious than this one. The unexpected comes out of the blue, and no matter how calm, prepared, or responsible we have been, there is a moment of panic when we have to deal with a reality we have never anticipated. For each, it is a different set of facts, but all have struggled in such moments.

A company is sold, and jobs disappear. A parent has to deal with the death of their child. A car runs a stop sign and crashes into your car. A friend, without explanation, will no longer return phone calls. A perfect marriage suddenly ends in divorce. Everyone knows what I am talking about.

What were the moments in your life when you had been caught by surprise? Were you able to instantly recover and adjust, did it take time to figure out a change in plan, or are you still in the midst of shock or recovery? Life is full of so many surprises.

When Jesus spent his last meal with his disciples on the night of his betrayal, they had no clue what was coming next. They arrived in Jerusalem to celebrate Passover, and the crowds loved the fact that Jesus was in their midst. There had been a parade, and excitement was building as all hoped he would proclaim himself Messiah, take the throne, and begin to bring all the hoped-for glory and peace they had waited so long to embrace.

The disciples treated the meal like a victory celebration, even as Jesus was facing a death they had no clue was coming. In the midst of that meal, John's Gospel shared a beautiful summary of Jesus's words as he prepared his disciples for a surprise that would shake them to their very core. He used the image of childbirth and labor, stating a woman has anxiety as the pain begins, but when the baby arrives, that struggle turns into joy. He promised his disciples of every age that his struggle would bring joy and peace to us in a similar fashion.

What a beautiful image! Everyone prepares for birth, but no one can prepare for all that happens in the struggle that is part of it. Jesus affirms that life will be full of such surprises, but his entrance into the fray is to assure us of his presence and power and the peace that he offers no matter what surprises we face. His comment "I have overcome the world" reminds us that no matter what we face, he has already dealt with it. And peace is the best way for people of faith to embrace, endure, and deal with each moment along the way. Faith brings peace, and peace brings a calm that changes surprise into patience and fear into the assurance of God's loving guidance.

We try so diligently to be prepared for each new day (as we have been taught in the Boy Scouts and by Mom and Dad). But surprise can overwhelm us so much with its suddenness that we can forget what is most important. That is the gift Jesus has talked about with his disciples and given to each of us—peace unlike anything the world can offer! The peace he lovingly offers is the calm of his presence, which allows us to take a deep breath, proceed with the next step, and know we are not alone.

DON'T WAIT

A YOUNG ARMY OFFICER, TWO years out of West Point, was assigned to serve in Japan after the end of the Second World War. He and his young wife were far away from family and friends but became close to some of the Lutheran pastors who had been sent as missionaries to Japan. The conflict in Korea broke out, and he was one of the first to be sent into that fray. His wife was pregnant with their first child and would deliver while he was in Korea. He received a battlefield promotion to captain several years before he would have even been considered for that rank. Then it was time to return to Japan, but his commander asked him to stay a few more months with the guarantee of promotion to major. Such a rank, just four years out of West Point, would have been unheard of, and he would have been far ahead of his peers in terms of rank. But his family was his life, and he passed on such an honor to rejoin his wife and young son. He gave up what many would pay for as his priorities were very clear.

At that end of this officer's career, he had orders to move to Germany and receive promotion to general. That would be the capstone of a successful career for a West Point graduate and ensure lucrative job offers in the civilian arena. He then received an offer for the Lutheran church as a business manager in the office that dealt with missions and missionaries. Because of his commitment to his faith, he gave up a promotion to general to work for the church. His church was his life. Within a few short years, conflict was inflicted within the Missouri Synod. A seminary faculty was fired, the pastor he worked for was dismissed, and he and the mission staff resigned in frustration at the conflict that was tearing a church body apart. Several years earlier, he would have been a general. Now he was unemployed—but not for long.

I am proud of my father and selfishly share a memory to make a point. He knew how much I loved him. I was blessed to spend much time with him during the decline of his health and his time of death. But I never told him along the way, while he and I could still have a good conversation, how proud he made me by those decisions that showed how priorities of faith and family had gifted my life. I was blessed by his example of how priorities guide decisions. In a world where success and fame seemed the goals of so many, his example enriched not only his family but also everyone who knew him well.

We all struggle with hindsight and the wishes that we should have said and done things differently or initiated conversations that are too late to engage in now. None of us are perfect, and we all have such baggage that can only be changed by the gift of God's forgiving love. We can't change what we can't change, but God frees us from those anchors dragging behind us. God's gift of forgiveness is indeed a freeing act of love.

Often, when Jesus told people he had set free to go and sin no more, we are reminded of a next step. We can't change what we can't change, but we do have control of what we do next.

I know because of my father's love for me and mine for him that it will be silly to wallow in what I should have told him but didn't. I also know I have learned from that and try more often to tell loved ones how I really feel rather than hold it back for a rainy day. And that is the point that I have maybe taken too long to get to in this reminiscence.

All of us have things we need to tell one another, especially those we love and can so easily take for granted. So often at funerals, I have suggested to families the importance of sharing stories about loved ones so children and grandchildren will know better about someone who is no longer around. But more important is not to wait until the time of death to remember and celebrate what is important. Why wait till later or put off for a more comfortable time what you can do and say today?

Take time to tell those you love and treasure why that is so. Don't make them assume anything. A simple thank-you is a gift that we need to share more often, rather than frustrations and fears that kindle so many arguments and misunderstandings. My dad knew how much I loved him, but I could have told him a few more things than I did. Each of you has similar regrets and opportunities. If there is someone who has touched you, changed you, filled you with admiration or respect, or given your life a new meaning or priority, don't wait to say "thank you" for that moment that is right before you, which may not be available again. And when you miss the moment, be assured of the power of grace and learn from what may have been missed.

Regrets are a dime a dozen, while love is a gift beyond value. One of the greatest lessons I am still learning is that love that is not shared now is love that is wasted. Don't put off till tomorrow what you can give today! As should be very obvious, my father's love continues to teach me today.

REMEMBER

WE ALL HAVE DIFFERENT PARENTING styles that may or may not reflect how we have been raised. As a child, I never understood that my parents weren't always certain of what was the best way to handle five children, each of whom was a unique personality with different moods and needs. In hindsight, I am amazed at how much better they were at their task than I had any clue of.

Now that I have had to deal with the protection, nurture, and development of my own children, I have come to understand even better how difficult a task my parents have had. A special gift at Christmas this year from my daughter has made me remember even more what a simple way my mom has found for such a difficult undertaking (for I was a handful, to say the least).

When I was in high school and would leave home for work, time with friends, or an occasional date, Mom's parting words (and only advice) was simply, "Remember whose you are." I have shared this often enough in sermons that others constantly remind me of the power that phrase has even for them. The beauty of such a simple reminder is the complexity of what is behind it. Whose am I? What a question that evokes. Am I a child of my parents? Or am I a child of God? Am I part of a family that is affected by my moods and actions? Am I my own person? And the answer is yes. But in my world and for my family, it has always begun with what happens at baptism and the bigger family and heavenly parent who has created me, gifted me, and set me free to live on planet Earth.

When I was in high school, I didn't think about all that and didn't even wonder what Mom meant. In fact, I am pretty sure I didn't understand the words at all, but I heard and remembered them. Somewhere deep inside it must have made a difference because those words hung over me when I was away from home, like the echo of a distant voice. And I always remembered even when I didn't understand.

This Christmas my daughter Abby gave me a leather-bound journal, and on the bottom corner was imprinted "EES" for Eunice Elaine Seeber, my mom. Underneath those initials, also imprinted, was "Remember Whose You Are." Having had to surrender my mother to heaven, I think about her all the time. I can still hear the love in her voice as if she were saying it again now. And now this journal will be a daily reminder never to forget the love given immeasurably to me.

When Mom moved into an independent living facility, one Christmas Rox and Abby decided to have a little wooden sign made that said, "Remember whose you are." We hung it in Mom's apartment. When she entered a care facility, my sisters put it in the shadow box by her door so every time Mom or any of us entered her room, we saw those words. They became the same reminder to Mom as they had been for so many years to me. And they were a reminder to her that we listened and were thankful for her gift to us. Remember!

That is the tone of the blessing I will never forget in my mom's simple gift to me. I share this knowing we all have different memories and realities in our own upbringing, and my intent is to share with you two thoughts. If we daily remember whose we are (and first we must reflect on what that means), it can change how we live and feel and act. At the same time, as I realize the simple way in which Mom has encapsulated the priorities of my life for me, I understand that what I say and do for others can have the same lasting impact (either good or bad). But the mirror of our mind keeps bringing us back to whatever is most important. I encourage all to begin with what is good and blessed and touched by God as the most important reflections, which can change us and also be the glimmer of light that others see in us.

All this came about because of Mom's little blessing. *Remember whose you are.* Why would I ever not want to remember, and how could I ever forget?

RELICS

WHEN WE VISITED VARIOUS CATHEDRALS, basilicas, and even little chapels throughout Europe, the tour guides always made certain we knew what specific relics of some saint were in the sanctuary. We saw altars with bones, pieces of cloth inside a gold-covered glass box, nails, pieces of wood, and even a thorn reputed to be from Jesus's crown of thorns behind glass. The cathedral in Cologne, Germany, had a reliquary that was said to contain the bones of the three wise men who visited the infant Jesus. Some called those relics holy.

Relics are important in drawing people into those places of worship and making a connection with the past. People even worship or pray to those relics, feeling that in their presence they are somehow closer to God. Whether any of those relics are actually what they are said to be is a discussion for another time. And the fact that they are important for some and ridiculed by others is not an issue for now either.

I simply ask you to consider the relics we surround ourselves with. My house is full of memorabilia from my parents or grandparents, such as baptism certificates, military insignia, diplomas, jewelry, and books from their elementary school they have written their names in. They are of no value to anyone but me, and I wonder why such relics are so important. For some reason they make me feel closer to someone whom I can't touch or see anymore. And they are more of a physical presence than a memory. These relics are special.

But I also hang on to old cameras I don't use anymore and duck decoys and oak furniture that have belonged to someone else but are from a period that is no longer here. Is this all about not letting go of the past, or in feeling closer to such relics, does that somehow give us connections that either keep us from feeling isolated or help us honor and celebrate those who have traveled this earthly highway before we have?

My wife will roll her eyes as she talks about T-shirts and suits I will never wear again but can't bear to let go of. Why do some of us have trouble letting go of what isn't really important but gives comfort and a sense of peace in being tied to something that was important in a different way at a different time? These relics are all called ordinary.

How do we decide what is so valuable it should be kept, and what do we keep that keeps us from moving on to the present and future? How do we keep relics from becoming more than they should be?

In cathedrals in Europe with valuable relics, the princes and kings competed with one another to claim they had more relics than someone else. Over time what might have been a reminder of a moment from scripture or the life of a sainted Christian, whose witness continues to inspire, sometimes moved from being a simple relic to an object of devotion and worship. We don't like to call that idolatry, do we? And yet it certainly gets pretty close, don't you think?

But maybe that is true with much of what I keep on my shelves or in my closet as well. If it becomes so important that it keeps me from adding new memories or more practical items, has it become more than a treasured keepsake? I am not always sure where to draw the line. We are foolish if we do not honor and respect the past and the special people and times that God has blessed our lives with. At the same time, if we cannot more forward and celebrate such giftedness by becoming a similar gift in the lives of others, are we missing the point of why our parents or a great woman or man of the past has been so special to us?

I have been wrestling all day with whether to write this as I don't want to offend anyone or disparage what is important as an aid to loving God or someone else in our lives. But from firsthand experience, I know that I have surrounded myself with many relics that can easily become more important and of value than they should. When I cannot let go of anything and that keeps me from moving on or giving similar attention, time, or love to someone who needs me right now, I know I have crossed a line that I would be better off not crossing.

It is no different from a hobby that becomes an obsession, a memory that I simply won't let go of, a friend who has hurt me so much that I just can't forgive, or a painful loss that keeps me from living with the joy and peace that Christ offers. There are relics, but there should be only one object of our worship and many present people and moments worthy of our time and our love. When Jesus talked about an unburied seed that would never bear fruit, I know he didn't have relics in mind, but maybe we should. Peace!

MESSENGERS

ROXANNE AND I WERE TALKING about our first dog, Nike. We had no fence, but she never left our yard. She would sit and watch kids or traffic but never crossed the border of our property line. That changed when Glen and Dee moved in next door. We became great friends. Either Nike sensed that or maybe it was because Glen was secretly feeding her scraps. If Nike wasn't in the yard, she was visiting Glen and Dee.

One night we decided to have some fun and see how smart Nike really was. I wrote a note asking Glen if he had any extra charcoal for my grill, stuffed it in Nike's collar, and told her to go see Glen. She wandered next door, and we sat in our lawn chairs and watched to see what would happen. We saw their back door open, and Nike went in. About ten minutes later, the door opened, and she came back to where we were sitting. She had a new note stuffed in her collar in which Glen said, "Yes, you can borrow charcoal, but some of the ribs will need to come back to me." A star was born. It did not involve as many moving parts as a long-ago message to Garcia, and yet for a dog, it was a fairly complicated task she performed perfectly.

Nike became a messenger as she walked with notes in her collar for Glen and back to us from him. And we had not had a dog since that would have even a clue of how to play the game. We miss Nike and Glen not because we no longer can send messages but because that has been such a special time in our lives.

In talking about Nike the messenger, it brought to mind a moment many years in the past. I was twelve, and we went to a weeklong Boy Scout camp with troops from all around the city. The climax of the week was the last night. It began with a sealed message that needed to be carried in a variety of ways as a relay race to the finish line. Each troop had separate teams for each segment of the race. The troop that won the race had bragging rights for the next year.

The first group gathered wood and stacked it for a fire. The second had to get the fire started with flint and steel. A rope was strung three feet over the fire, and when it burned through, a runner headed around the lake with the message. On the far side, it was opened by another team, who used Morse code to send it to another team, who wrote it down and gave it to a team who paddled a canoe across the lake. The message was given to the last runner, who ran the circumference of the lake with the message.

The first team to get the message delivered to the judge was the winner and received a special ribbon for their troop flag. It was a lot of fun, with much yelling and screaming, and a fitting way to end the week at camp. It was typical of the kinds of ways teamwork was learned. The relay involved many skills, teamwork, and getting the right guys for the right part of the relay for us to even have a chance. There were so many places along the way where the message could have gotten stalled, misplaced, mistranslated, or lost. As I think about it so many years later, it was amazing any of us actually got the race completed, but we did.

As I remembered that single relay message for all, I was drawn to consider the similarity with the many books of the Bible, written over a period of a thousand years by many different and inspired writers. This might seem a weird segue, but consider how many ways the message could have gotten off track, scrambled, or lost. Yet thousands of years since the oral traditions were written onto individual scrolls and kept in many different synagogues, monasteries, and churches, we still have the texts today. From Genesis to Revelation, the message is consistently the same. I never thought about the Bible's construction as being like a relay race, but in a sense it was.

Moses and the prophets shared God's message to them in words and by how they lived. Parents and grandparents memorized the words from God and shared them every night, sitting around the evening meal or campfire. Later, other prophets wrote parts of the message on scrolls. Then came letters from Paul and the precious Gospels. Monks and scribes copied scroll after scroll so the message could be passed from village to village and country to country. And then came the printing press! For hundreds and hundreds of years, faithful people were inspired by God to share the same message of God's loving purpose and promise. Because so many didn't keep silent, we have those words in our heads and hearts today.

What next? Who will be the next messengers to intentionally share the good news with loved ones and strangers alike? For God so loved the world he sent his Son—we know those words and take them to heart. And now it is for you and me to be the messengers for generations yet to be born. In Bible study and prayer, in worship and fellowship with other believers, the words of God become more and more a part of our daily lives. We are the next batch of messengers, and we have so many ways to let others know why Christmas and Easter are more than holidays, and the love of God is real and alive and for all! We are the next in line to continue the relay that brings light to the world.

ASSUMPTIONS

BECAUSE DAD WAS IN THE army, we lived in Germany for three years when I was a child. I was too young then to understand all that had happened during World War II or the Cold War that was underway in 1958. I was only in second grade when we arrived in Germany, so I was really too young to know much about anything! My concerns, as with any eight-year-old, had primarily to do with me.

Most of the military families lived in the same apartment complex. Our primary forms of entertainment were baseball, riding bikes, Saturday matinees at the theater, visits to castles, and the playground behind our apartment building. With no television, we spent more time on the playground than anywhere else. We had swing sets and slides, and we guarded them with a passion. Once, we took army surplus tents and sleeping bags and slept on the playground (until it was dark, and we got scared and went back into the apartments).

That was our turf! One day a few German kids living across the street came to use our playground. But it was our playground, and there were enough of my friends around, so we chased them away. It is embarrassing to even talk about it now as I understand dynamics that I had no clue of then. My parents were oblivious of what we were up to, or they would have explained to us the facts of life. We were just being selfish kids, too big for our britches, and afraid of encounters with other kids who didn't speak our language and looked a little scary. How little did I really know! Now that Mom and Dad are in heaven, it is easier to write about this as I won't face the embarrassment of having them read this. But it has been on my mind for many years.

A few years back, I was talking to Mom about our time in Giessen, and I asked about the kids from across the street. She explained they were refugees from Eastern Europe. They had been pushed out by the Russians and forced to live in a relocation camp that happened to be across the street from our apartments. With that fact and a more mature realization that we were visitors in their part of the world, I had a totally different take on that time of my life.

We were as innocent and naïve as any eight-year-old boys could be. But knowing what I know now, it doesn't make me feel any better about what had happened. Those kids had lost their homes, and some of them possibly had lost members of their families. We were living in a country that had been ravaged by war, but we had no sense of any of that. It wasn't my fault or that of my friends. We just didn't understand yet the facts of life. Of course, I regretted the selfishness that came with being a child. It was just one of those things that probably wasn't as big a deal as I had allowed it to be, and yet it had become an important teaching moment for me as an adult.

It brought to mind Saint Paul's words to young Christians in Corinth as he reflected on his own growth. When he was a youngster, he thought and acted like a child, but as an adult, he had to give up childish patterns and ways. He used that image to encourage our faith journey as our path to maturity developed.

Paul's point was that without Christ we are like children, with an inability to understand the finer points of God's plan for our living. Without the gift of faith our vision is clouded by selfishness, naivety, arrogance, and sometimes even evil. But having been blessed with the gracious gifts of Christmas and Easter, we now see our lives and the world around us with a clarity that only God can bring. Yet we are not perfect, and even many of our best efforts and intentions can fall short of what we hope for or what we are capable of.

How often have we made assumptions about others, only to learn later how misinformed we have been or how hurtful our thoughts and actions have become? How often have we thrown roadblocks or inflicted punishments on others without first truly understanding the facts at hand? Our world is so good at dividing, sewing suspicion, and teaching selfishness. That is the brokenness we call sin and the cloudy vision that has cleared up for Paul with his revelation that Jesus is Lord.

With clear vision comes a clearer purpose. As we will soon move out of the darkness of winter and into the bluer skies and warmer days of spring, it may serve as another reminder of the change that the love of Jesus can bring not only into our hearts but also into our actions. We are called to move from darkness to light, from the shadows into the clear sailing of servant love.

As children, we haven't had the experience or maturity to understand the nuances of life. As adults, we have no excuse to live like children. Surrounded by so many who have temper tantrums, create wars and divisions, and refuse to associate with others who are different, we understand the potential of the Gospel to bring the only real change the world can benefit from.

I am sorry for mistakes that I now understand. But unless I learn not to make the same mistakes again, my regret is shallow and nothing but hollow words. It is time for the light to shine and the love to flow, for that is who we have been redeemed, reclaimed, and empowered to be. And if we cannot teach the children of all ages by our actions, what value is there in our words about faith?

Paul had it right when he pointed out the three greatest gifts of faith, hope, and love and announced that the greatest of these is love!

HELP

ONE YEAR OF SEMINARY TRAINING was spent as a vicar, working full-time in a parish. Mine was in Miami, Florida. The pastor of this small congregation left for another congregation soon after I arrived, so I became pastor for the last months of my year and felt pretty grown up! Soon after he left, he called, asking a favor. He officiated the marriage of young Cubans a few months earlier. They were in trouble and called him for help. He called me, and he asked if I would give them a call.

That led into an interesting and somewhat troubling situation. They were younger than I was and scared to death, being convinced someone had placed a curse on them. They felt someone was jealous of their marriage and had gone to a voodoo priest to find a way to break them apart.

This was not something any of my seminary classes had touched on, so I was on my own. I asked why they thought a spell had been cast on them. They said on their honeymoon cruise, their wedding rings had both changed from gold to a murky gray. I had a spooky feeling at first but wondered if they had simply been victims of someone selling rings that really weren't gold in the first place.

Before I could share my wisdom, the bride told me that the day after they returned from their cruise, they heard a strange sound at their front door. They opened it to find a dead chicken hanging from the doorframe. They were scared to death and feared a disaster for one or both of them was imminent. I didn't have a clue what to say. The girl had moved back with her parents, and the guy said he was in hiding. They were genuinely filled with terror. They said there were voodoo priests in their neighborhood, and they needed to find some way to have this curse broken.

I asked them to give me a day to see what I might figure out and to come back the next afternoon. I had goosebumps after they left. When we are ready to start flexing our wings and go out on our own, which is what my situation happened to be, we are pretty certain we can conquer the world. This complicated my confidence, and I started feeling the same fear they did. What if such things could happen? What did I know about refugees from Cuba and Haiti and what was happening in some of their communities? Sometimes there is only one response to such difficult dilemmas, and that is to ask for help.

For a twenty-four-year-old who is feeling his oats, wearing a pastor collar, and ready to change the world, it is not easy to admit he needs help. But I finally admitted I was not as smart or prepared as I could have pretended, so I spent some time in prayer and then decided to ask for help. This could have been such an ego trip for me to make classmates envious of such an interesting moment and how I had ridden to the rescue. But prayer helped me get over myself and admit I was in over my head and needed to ask for help (not an easy decision but the right one). I called a pastor I knew who had a Cuban congregation in Little Havana. I explained what was up and that I needed his advice and help.

He explained that there was a religion in some neighborhoods known as Santeria. It is a blend of primitive African beliefs in a variety of spirits or gods and Roman Catholicism. Slaves brought to the Caribbean from Africa have blended two sets of beliefs into one. Animal sacrifice is a big part of this religion. The pastor told me of a Catholic priest who had done a lot of work with such situations. I called him, we met, and he explained much about Santeria and his work with those who had been caught in its influence. I was even more scared and glad I had not tried to play lone ranger on this one. He agreed to meet with the couple, and they were willing to talk to him. I never heard from them again, so I don't know how their problems were resolved, but that was fine with me.

This has been an important learning moment for me. Sometimes there are situations we are not capable of dealing with. When there is an illness, that is easy. Go see a doctor. When a car quits running, it is easy. Take it to a mechanic. But often, we don't know what to do or are too stubborn to admit we are in over our head. Sometimes we want to just hide under a blanket and hope what is troubling just goes away. And there are moments in which we either don't know we need help or are too arrogant to ask. That is why so many marriages fail, friendships are lost, and mistakes are made that never need to have happened. And often, just asking for help will have led to a better fix.

We are daily surrounded by darkness, disappointment, grief, and other situations beyond our ability to manipulate or control. When we are willing to admit our weakness, fears, or confusion about what to do next, the most important thing to do is to ask for help. And for people of faith, that begins with prayer. When we entrust such issues into God's hands and really let them go, that is the beginning of help that is beyond what we can achieve on our own.

Throughout his ministry, Jesus would disappear to a quiet place to pray. As he began his ministry, he spent forty days in the wilderness prayerfully asking for help. As he faced his arrest, he prayed for help. Let that be an example and reminder of how we might deal with those scary, tough moments in life. When admitting the need and asking for help is our beginning, we are more open to the answers that God will always provide. Often, help comes best when we are willing to listen, to watch, and to learn. Don't ever be afraid to ask for help, and always remember: God is our first place to go.

PATIENCE

OUR CURRENT BEAGLE IS NAMED Bosco. The first three years of his life, he has been a laboratory dog in a research setting, living by himself, in a cage. SPCA rescues such dogs and finds real homes for them, similar in a lesser way to Moses leading slaves out of Egypt to freedom!

We anticipated issues would emerge for Bosco as he began to experience normal doggy moments and living in freedom rather than a cage. Grass, snow, and running with other dogs in a fenced-in dog park were some of his new joys. I assumed the learning curve would be for Bosco rather than me. Wrong!

Dogs and I do well together as their affection is less conditional than for humans. Bosco and I walk every morning and afternoon. He is acting more and more like a normal dog with one exception—his relationship with me. For some reason, especially in the evening, all bets are off. He can act as if he is afraid of me or doesn't remember who I am. (I thought I deserved better! Ha!)

This confounds me as I want for him to play or wag his tail in greeting, but he doesn't do that (for me). He has been a great addition and is totally in love with Roxanne. When she comes home, he sits like a rabbit, wags his tail, and waves his paws. When she goes to the back door to call him in from the yard, he comes in (well, after a few attempts). When I go to the door, he runs to the back fence as if I were the scariest critter he has ever seen.

Sound familiar? When you cannot get someone to pay attention to you or respond as you want, how do you feel? How do you deal with the frustration, anger, or confusion when such disappointments make no sense? What goes through your mind when you are alone and would rather not be? We know such feelings all too well, and no one ever gets used to them. We appreciate quiet moments when they are on our terms but are confused when we are ready for attention and it doesn't come the way we hoped for.

It is frustrating for me to see Bosco asleep on the couch in the evening, nuzzling with Roxanne, only to run away like a scared rabbit when I walk in the room. None of us deal with rejection well, do we? None of us enjoy it when friends no longer are or when someone we want to be close to isn't interested in getting to know us. These are all life issues we can struggle with.

In my case, I need to remember Bosco is going to be what he is going to be. For me to force the issue with him will not have a good ending for either of us. And it isn't fair as I have no way of knowing what has conditioned him this way. I know it isn't about me and need to not make it be about me. (Deep breath!)

One evening after another of his mad dashes out of the room when I passed by, I took a different approach. I waited until he settled on the couch, then quietly sat on the other side. I said nothing, sat still, and closed my eyes for a while. When I opened them, as expected, he was watching me closely. I slowly started scratching his ear, which he always liked, then just closed my eyes again and sat quietly. After about twenty minutes, I left the room. I'd keep it up.

I can't force him to act the way I want. He is too conditioned by his previous surroundings. But trying to spend more time on his turf in the evening, being patient and letting him watch and wonder what I am up to may help him tolerate my presence. (And it may calm me down as well.) He may even worry less about whatever it is that I stir up in his little doggy brain of memories as there is no way to know what his life has been like living in a cage in a laboratory setting.

He is capable of great affection, as evidenced in his bonding with Roxanne. Rather than complain such happiness isn't directed to me, I need to celebrate what he has found that he probably has never had before now. He will do what he will do, and my worry will not help, just like in other life moments! The only person I can control is me, and my attempts to control others may seem successful on the surface but can lead to other issues that will only appear somewhere else. Therein is the lesson to be learned.

In our relationships we are often disappointed or hurt when others do not act as we wish, respond as we hope, or give what we need. We never have any way of knowing the full story or whether that is even their intent. Just because I want someone to like me doesn't mean they need to. My expectations may not even be fully understood by them. At the same time, when someone reaches out to me, I will do better to remember how I have felt when ignored.

Without a doubt, Bosco is acting out of something in his past. He will need time to learn that his fears are unfounded. Until he does, it makes no sense to feel as if his actions are about me, which they likely are not. Better to find joy in my life, and his, rather than complain about what I can't understand and should probably not try to control. Meaningful and true love among and between people is like that.

Sometimes stepping back rather than complaining or imposing new pressures is the greatest gift we can offer! And it can even bring peace on both sides of the fence! Christ has not taught us to demand what we want but to give what will help show selfless and forgiving love.

And along the way, a day has come at the vet when Bosco has actually jumped up to sit in my lap. So maybe I am better off being patient and celebrating good moments rather than being offended when things don't go the way I desire. Just maybe!

REFLECTIONS

OUR CULTURE IS FASCINATED WITH lifting others as role models to be adored and honored. How about you? Have you ever set out to imitate someone? Has another person ever tried to imitate you? Are you sure? How will that make you feel, or will it depend on what they have copied?

We all are shaped by people, situations, and choices. We reflect what is important (or not) in our lives. Sometimes we are aware of that, and other times we are not, but we are in so many ways the reflections or antireflections of others. Some decisions are conscious, and we have no control over others. Our parents, birthplaces, and the homes we have grown up in are not of our choosing, but in other segments of our life, either by choice or rebellion, we follow the examples, guidance, or lure of others we want to emulate.

In my first congregation, our neighbors had twins. Their house had a detached garage. The driveway was right next to the twins' bedroom. Dad and his buddies from the GM plant spent weekends on that driveway working on cars. Dad and Mom were concerned that the twins were three years old but didn't talk. They babbled in baby talk with each other but nothing their parents could understand.

One day the mom happened to quietly pass by the bedroom when she thought her darling daughters were asleep but heard the girls using every four-letter word from the factory floor where Dad worked! They were imitating Dad and his friends but not in the way Dad and Mom hoped. The men didn't realize what role models they were or what the twins were learning from them. Oops!

We live with reflections. The color of leaves is reflected light. Our children's tantrums are reminders of what we have been like at that age. Our eyes take everything in, and our brain processes the information. As we look around and see how others act and live, whose reflections are the ones we embrace?

How often do we stop, look, and consider what each of us reflects to those around us. It is like a mirror inviting us to take a time from daily routines and look more closely at the servant love Jesus models, asking, "How would this look like on me?" Jesus surrendered an eternity in heaven to spend a brief, few years on the earth to look like us, get our attention, and hope we might mirror his reflection of God's plan for us through our own faith, hope, and love. He even surrendered that earthly life so he could join us in death. Jesus came into our world to introduce a new role model for us to reflect. Consider, if you will, the intensity and blessing of such a loving surrender!

Through his life, death, and resurrection, Jesus has changed the shape and appearance of creation forever. He has taken the broken and made it whole, taken the lost and said it is found, embraced those who feel lonely and given them unconditional love, taken death and given it life. He calls us to see his image superimposed on ours as we look in the mirror.

Just because we avoid a mirror doesn't mean there is no image, for a mirror always reflects something whether we like it or not. If we hold up a mirror and the image is only of ours, we do well to remember the word about graven images or idolatry. As we lift the miracle mirror of grace, we see instead an image that has changed us or our new mirror image of faithful love. In other words, God helps us become the reflections of the One we love!

A few years ago, I read a wonderful story about the jazz great Wynton Marsalis. What he could do with a trumpet most musicians could only dream of. He was playing in one of the premiere jazz clubs in New York. He started a haunting solo that over time grew quieter, slower, simpler until if finally finished with a few quiet notes and silence in between. No one moved. They sat in in silent rapture and awe. He was incredible. He had their attention! And then as a dramatic conclusion, he prepared to end the silence with one last perfect note.

But like a broken mirror, someone's cell phone shattered the moment!

Time stopped. The audience was stunned. The moment was ruined. Marsalis looked around silently. For everyone it was an awkward moment, until slowly he put his trumpet back to his lips and slowly, quietly imitated the tone of the cell phone. He played it over and over again, taking the brokenness of that phone that interrupted his love song. And through his amazing gift, those tones gradually changed to mirror his original tune. Before anyone had realized what he was doing, he was back on the tune he had started with and finished as he had done before! Again, it was followed by hushed silence. It was a miracle moment!

Then the crowd went wild as they realized what he had done. He had changed what was broken, embraced it, made it part of a beautiful tune, and creatively finished the song he began with.

That should sound like a familiar theme for all of us. Think about the horrified silence at the cross and empty tomb and how the disciples gradually realized what Jesus had done as he took our broken lives, changing the tone of our living and the tune of our dying, and recreated each of us into a song of love that might indeed mirror his—in other words, reflections of the One we love!

THE LEAP OF FAITH

I ENJOY TEACHING AS IT helps me learn and grow. In a morning Bible study with men, we cover many topics of faith as taught in the Bible but always from the perspective of how these inspire our living. What is always most powerful for me are the insights and experiences others offer.

In a recent discussion, we were looking at a story in John's Gospel of the healing of a young man who was blind from birth. It was difficult for most of us to imagine what it would be like to suddenly be able to see when that had never even been a possibility. The drama of such a miracle was overshadowed, however, by the attacks of Jesus's critics as the man who was healed was bombarded with questions about whether he had even been blind in the first place in an attempt to discredit Jesus. This took the concept of shooting the messenger to a new low! A young man knew he was healed, and in being forced to wrestle with how it happened, he came to a place of incredible faith and became the teacher rather than the victim his critics wanted to paint him as.

We discussed the progression of faith in this young man as he moved from blindness to truly seeing Jesus for who he is. In doing so, it sounds so much like our process of life, from infancy to maturity. Life begins with all that is needed, but we must grow into it. Life is our gift, and we grow into it. So it is with faith; it is fully endowed, and we all grow into faith in different stages and different ways.

One member of our class had a military background. Part of his training was a time in jump school, which meant parachuting out of airplanes. I asked him if when he jumped out of an airplane, that was a moment for him when faith became real. The question just popped out. I had no idea why I asked other than thinking about what it would take for me to jump out of a plane and trust that I would live. He surprised me with his response. He said that faith was not an issue until about the sixth jump. And then he explained.

He said the first four jumps were exciting. But on his fifth jump, his main chute malfunctioned. The emergency chute thankfully worked, but the next time he had to go up, he said he had never been so scared in all his life. He was dreading that jump but had no choice and knew he had to jump. (And I couldn't even imagine what that felt like!)

As the plane was climbing to altitude, he sat with all his paratrooper buddies as they were ready to go and just waiting for the order to jump! He told us that in that moment, he was filled with an incredible sense of peace. He knew he was where he needed to be and was doing what he was called to do. He felt he had complete trust in God no matter what happened. That moment was described by him as a time of peace.

He told us that was a moment when he really felt the power of faith and never looked back. Now to be sure, this was not the first moment of faith but a moment where faith was more than a word or concept, and he was privileged to feel its presence and the assurance and peace it offered.

Many years ago, I had a running conversation about faith with one of our very active members. She felt faith is something that grows and worried about how she could make her faith stronger. Our conversations were helpful to both of us in different ways. Everyone wonders from the same perspective about whether we have enough faith, especially when we face a crisis or difficulty in life. That is when faith needs to be real, and it is easy to panic before having a willingness to trust what we cannot see or prove.

Jesus's words to his disciples consistently promised his gift of peace. He does the same for us so that no matter what the fear or worry, we are offered the presence of his peace. This is God's gift, not something we deserve or can earn. It is beyond what we can explain or understand. That is why we call it faith.

On my office wall, I have a wonderful framed reminder of that gift. It says, "When you come to the edge of all the light you know and are about to step off into the darkness of the unknown, faith is knowing one of two things will happen: There will be something solid to stand on or you will be taught how to fly."

It is in the leap we call faith we always find peace!

LETTING GO

THE TIME HAS ARRIVED IN my life when I need to start cleaning out my office. My bookcases are full of books that have been so important that I've bought them. Many of them I have used over and over again. Many have not been opened in over twenty years. But I hang on to them all, just in case I may need them someday. But the collection seems to keep growing and growing, and I have to admit I just don't like to let go of my things. It is difficult for me to let go.

We all are like that to a certain extent. Do you remember, as children, how excited we were to find a beautiful butterfly or a caterpillar more colorful and fuzzier than we had ever seen? Maybe you found a toad or a frog. And we always did the same thing. We got a jar, filled it with grass or weeds, and dropped our valuable discovery inside. Then we poked holes in the lid so our prize could breathe, and we had something special to share. Maybe it went with us to school on a day for show-and-tell, and maybe it just stayed on the shelf in our bedroom so we could watch it every day. And the same thing often happened. If we hung on to it too long, it died. That was never part of the plan and brought about some of the first feelings of guilt many of us encountered as we realized it was our fault!

We all have times when it is difficult for us to let go of what is near and dear, especially when it is someone whom we love and cannot imagine being without. How difficult was it for you when your firstborn child left home? Or a marriage ended? Or a parent died? There are moments in which we refuse to let go. And the pain of even considering such a move is more than we can bear.

Many years ago, I had to face the reality that my wife was dying. It was the most difficult moment in my life that I had ever faced, and I was not ready for what was coming next. I didn't want to admit it was happening, and I couldn't imagine it was anything more than a terrible dream. And yet I kept waking up to the same reality. I was going to be alone, and that was not something I could imagine or wanted to face.

She was incredible in how she helped all her family and friends to deal with what she couldn't escape. Her faith gave her courage beyond anything I had ever witnessed, and her love gifted me more than I deserved. And the lessons I learned from that time must be shared as that helped bring something positive out of a terrible and painful moment.

She and I had a big argument one day, and it had to do with the idea of letting go. She said she knew she was dying, and that moment was getting near. She said it was becoming more difficult for her to face because I wouldn't let her go. I couldn't believe what she was saying. I understood, but I couldn't let go. My response was that when the time came, I would let go, but I wasn't ready! And I'd never forget what she said next.

She said it wasn't up to me when that time would come. She told me I was not failing her by letting go. It was not my fault, and it was not her desire. But it was coming soon. I thought love meant I had to hold her tighter than I ever had before, but she was telling me something totally different. She said, "If you really love me, you have to let me go."

I still can't believe that conversation, but I am so thankful for the love that has inspired it. She was tired. She was ready for heaven. But she was worried about her family and needed me to do what I had to do. She needed to know that I would accept what was happening whether I liked it or not. I thought I was showing love by holding on so tight, and she said it was in letting go that my love would give her the peace that she needed.

Jesus had helped his disciples prepare for his own death with similar words as he used the example of planting a seed. He said only by letting go and planting that seed, where it could not be seen, could it achieve its potential. It had to be buried in the earth so that it could later sprout and bear fruit.

It is only in Jesus's death that we can have life. It is in surrender that faith takes over where our control fails. If God can change death by his surrender and letting go of what we hang on to so dearly, then life takes on a new power and joy that will be impossible without that great surrender.

My wife's death did not have the same power as that of Jesus, and yet it had the power that Jesus's life and death and resurrection brought about. And she shared that surrender of faith with me and helped me see that in letting go, I was, in fact, showing greater love than I could muster on my own. As she taught me about the surrender of faith, she helped me grow into my faith so that it was more than a concept or words but an existence that gave me life in the midst of death.

Many of you have been blessed in your journey by others as I have been. In sharing what I have learned about surrender of faith, I pray that her gift to me will be a gift to you. She has been like that, and such sharing guides me to understand why letting go has helped me grow.

BELIEVE

GROWING UP IN AN ARMY family, we moved so often I could remember few of the names of my teachers as I saw them one year and never again. But I could remember my ninth-grade science teacher in Kansas, Mr. Barnes. He was a challenge and an enigma, not because he was a tough teacher but because we were never certain about whether he was giving us fact or fiction. For instance, in our class on genetics and mutation, one session was the observation of tiny fruit flies. We used microscopes to see the difference in their eye colors and so forth to learn how the combination of genetic codes from each parent resulted in what made each one different or the same. So far, so good.

But then the fun started. Mr. Barnes told us our fruit flies were Mediterranean. (I checked on the internet, and there really is such a species.) He said they migrated every spring across the Atlantic from the Mediterranean Sea and came to Kansas. Then in the fall, he told us, they then migrated back to France, Spain, Turkey, and Greece and spent winters there. That fact was not part of our test but was what I remembered best. Being an army brat, I had such a respect for authority that my tendency was to believe without any reservation anything an adult told me. He knew we were all like that, and as you could tell, he had fun from time to time. It was harmless except we believed him.

On another day he told us every one of us was born with a tail. (It had to be from that same unit on genetics and evolution.) He said doctors kept it a secret, but at birth they cut off babies' tails so no one would ever know we had one. He suggested that if we felt the end of our tailbone, we could feel where the tail had been connected. There was no way we dared ask Mom or Dad, for it was obviously a secret only adults knew about. Good old Mr. Barnes. Now you know why I have never forgotten his name.

It is interesting to me how easily we can be ripe for such deceptions or misdirection. There is no doubt in my mind that he was just having fun with us, was probably bored in his job, and liked a good laugh. But as I think about it now, we still have that tendency today to believe without question what we are told if it is from a source we have decided is credible and has our best interests in mind. I don't want to get too specific as it is too easy to slip into a discussion that may wind up dividing us because of political or social realities. But you know what I mean. There are some people, sources, or truisms that we will believe without question when sometimes a simple question will reveal to us that we have been had. How often have we believed in something too good to be true, only to later discover that it is indeed too good to be true?

As I look back and realize how gullible I have been, it is embarrassing, but I don't mind admitting how silly that is. Fruit flies only live a month, and it will be impossible for something that tiny to fly so far. My spine has to end somewhere, and so it does. Regardless of anything else, I know doctors don't cut tails off babies when they are born. But at a time, I have wondered if he is right.

Mr. Barnes was simply having fun. He likely also wanted us to begin to learn about critical thinking but should have probably been teaching kids older than adolescents, who were terrified of adults and gullible to a fault. (Times have changed, right?) As I thought about that classroom, I wondered if that was the same kind of issue that got Adam and Eve into trouble in the garden. They thought they had the facts straight, and then came the curveball and the challenge "You do know, don't you, that God is holding stuff back from you?"

We all struggle with such questions every day of our lives. What will we accept by faith, and what will we challenge with our human wisdom or miss because of the weakness called gullibility? For instance, when there is a tragic murder, is there an easy solution, or is there more involved that goes deeper than the facts as presented? When a marriage fails, is it obviously the fault of one or the other, or may there be other issues that even the principals involved are not even aware of? Sometimes we get real facts, and sometimes we get curveballs. Life is not perfect; the brokenness of sin means that people lie to suit their own means or misdirect us for some sort of selfish or perverse gain on their part.

As children of God, before we begin to deal with any other issue, it is our surrender called faith that should influence thoughts and actions. What that means is we know whose we are, what we are created for, how God's love has shaped us, and how we are called to shape how we touch life around us. Having surrendered to God and knowing we are in his loving protection and guidance no matter what, we have a much easier path to travel. We begin with the most important facts cemented by faith. As we then respond to the difficult questions and opportunities of a complicated and selfish world, we know we are loved and called to love. That allows us to start sorting, gathering, planning, and living, knowing as well that forgiveness will lift us when we fail, and God's love will keep guiding and guarding.

Sometimes easy answers aren't the right ones, and the easy path is not the right track. Other times the wind may blow in a different direction. But the bottom line is simple: if God is your love and life, your life will more often be guided and led by the same love that offers peace that the world cannot give and a future nothing on the earth can create. Believe what you believe, and understand that is what will guide what comes next.

MIAMI CHRONICLE

MY YEAR OF VICARAGE (INTERNSHIP) to gain practical experience in ministry was spent in Miami, Florida. The congregation was small and located at the main road into downtown. Homeless people slept on our lawn and daily asked for help. Next door was a motel frequented by ladies of the night. This was quite an introduction to ministry! A month later, my supervising pastor left to become pastor of a church in Ohio. To say I was wet behind the ears was being kind. Most often, I was like a deer frozen in the headlights of an approaching car.

I was usually alone as Sunday mornings were the only time anyone was in the building. Saturday afternoons were sermon-writing time as my wife worked second shift at a local hospital. My office was at the rear of the building.

One Saturday I heard a knock. I opened the door to find a confused, disheveled elderly man whose speech impediment was so severe I had no clue what he was saying. My first impulse was to push him away, lock the doors, and call the police. But I brought him in. And boy was I in for a surprise!

He sat down on the other side of my desk. My chair was next to the door, so I felt safe and knew I could escape quickly if necessary. I couldn't tell if he was confused, mentally disturbed, or one of the regulars who slept under the tropical vegetation of our lawn. Attempting a conversation with a confused man with a severe speech impediment was not something any of my counseling or pastoral care courses had prepared me for. To say I was nervous was an understatement.

He kept trying to tell me something and seemed to get more agitated as he talked. Twice, I excused myself from the office, telling him I needed to check something, and went out into the sanctuary with the hope he might just leave. I prayed and came back in. No such luck; he was still there. This scenario repeated itself for about twenty minutes, even though it seemed like hours. Finally, he pulled out his wallet and pointed at it like I was supposed to do something with it. There was no cash, only a social security check with a name and address on it. I asked if this was his, and he nodded yes. But I still had no clue what he wanted or what I could do.

As it was before the advent of internet and cell phones, everything happened at a snail's pace, and patience was more a given than it is today. After a while, I told him I needed to leave the office again and used that moment to mumble another prayer, go to the secretary's office, make a phone call to the town in North Carolina on his check, and see if directory assistance could help me locate someone from his family. I couldn't remember how long it took, but I finally found a listing with the same last name. To make a long story short, I made a phone call and wound up talking with his daughter.

The man had been in and out of a VA hospital and was currently living with his daughter. She said, years earlier, he had been severely injured in an accident and was suffering from dementia. He had wandered away from home the day before. She had been frantically looking for him and had no clue how he had gotten to Miami. Obviously, he couldn't tell me that either, but we were finally able to begin to see a possible solution to what was going on.

I called the police, explained what was going on, and asked if they could pick him up and find a way to get him on a bus. I had called traveler's aid (I don't even know if such organizations exist anymore), but it was Saturday, and no one answered. I didn't have any cash, my wife had the car at work, and I had no clue what a bus ticket would cost. I called the bus station, and they said they would accept his social security check for a bus ticket home, and I gave them the address his daughter had shared and wrote it out for the man as well. My heart was racing as I was excited about maybe getting him out of my office and out of town. I went back and started a long wait for the cops to show up.

Throughout this entire episode, he seemed agitated and kept mumbling.

I tried to act more interested than afraid. He didn't seem dangerous, just confused, and after talking to his daughter, I felt more secure and hoped he would stay put until the police arrived. As I sat down behind the desk, a new surprise awaited as the gentlemen stood up, took off his shirt, and pointed to a large scar on his abdomen. Then he started to take off his shoes. His mumbling kept me from understanding what he was trying to tell me. All I could think of was what cops would think if they walked into the office at that moment. I told him to put his shirt back on and sit down as help was on the way. And I said another silent prayer! He gradually settled down, and several minutes later, the police arrived. Finally!

The police took him to the bus station. I called his daughter and said a prayer of thanks that he was safe and I would not be the subject of any stories in the Miami newspapers the next day.

So what is the point? Maybe it is a reminder we can never be completely prepared for the unknown. Or sometimes we simply have to do the best we can with situations that occur and just let life happen. This moment has helped me learn that life is often full of surprises, we can only do the best we can, and prayers are always the best help when we don't know what else to do. And oh yeah, miracles do happen every day, often when we least expect! Life is not always clean and easy, yet knowing we are never alone calms us on our journey. That is not part of the curriculum the seminary has intended but, obviously, one God has walked me through—just as he does with each of you. Life can surprise, but faith never disappoints. We are never alone!

BABY STEPS

A BABY BIRD TAUGHT ME a lesson that should be so easy to remember but was so easy to forget. This year it was not robins but house finches that laid eggs in our hanging basket of flowers on the porch. We were getting used to losing one basket each year to the needs of nesting birds as they pretty much destroyed the flowers with their nest building and constant pooping.

The birds hatched about two weeks ago, and one had already disappeared. They were too little to fly and still had all those puffy beginnings of feathers that made them look twice as large as their parents. When I got home yesterday, the male was feeding the remaining baby bird (which was a good life lesson for dads to remember). But that was incidental to the lesson of the day. When I went out later, I noticed the nest was empty. I looked around to see if the little guy had fallen out as I knew he was not ready to fly.

Then I noticed him sitting on the mulch under our maple tree in the front yard, not moving, just standing still. The parent birds were flying back and forth and making quite a fuss as he just sat on the ground. His wings were not ready for him to fly, and he was now ripe to be found by a cat or a bigger bird.

I had garden gloves on and gently picked him up and put him back in the basket. Not knowing if he was ready to leave the nest or not, I thought it would at least offer a few hours to figure things out. The parent birds settled down, and he stayed put all afternoon. Whether that was the right thing to do wasn't the issue. I just felt the need to help.

But it made me realize something that was easy to forget. I only did little, but at least I felt it was right, and it was a problem I could deal with. Too often, the issues that wind us up seem beyond our control to change, and our efforts end in frustration rather than peace. What I remembered with that little bird was that sometimes it is better to do a little deed within our control rather than be frustrated by what is beyond our reach.

I have remembered what I forget too often. It is often the little things, the simple deeds, the unnoticed actions, the unrewarded successes, and the peace that comes from simply doing the best we can do whether anyone else is aware of it or not. All too often, we try to do too much or focus on situations so global in scope that any effort of ours is like trying to stop a wave from crashing on the beach or ending the conflict in the Middle East. We focus so much on the endgame, which is beyond our ability to control, that we wind up paralyzed and doing nothing.

Life can be overwhelming like that. Rather than be overwhelmed by moments and movements beyond quick fixes, sometimes a smile for someone who is sad, a conversation with someone who is lonely, or even a brief prayer can be just as helpful as a thousand-dollar donation to a favorite cause or waiting for a miracle beyond what we are capable of.

Sometimes the simple things are the most important, which is easy to forget in a world of headlights and headlines. Most of the time it is the little things that make the biggest difference of all. It has taken a little bird to remind me of what I so easily forget.

RUNAWAY

WE HAVE ALL SEEN OR heard of people having a near-death experience as their life flashes before their eyes. It makes for gripping drama in books and movies and not-so-amusing moments for those in the midst of a crisis or accident. Such moments of panicked reflection happen not only in the most critical of times but also often when there is anything traumatic that catches us off guard and we are uncertain of our emotional survival. One way or another, whether we have experienced such a moment or not, we understand the complicated scenario this describes. I had one such moment, more amusing in hindsight but just as terrifying while it happened. Bosco the beagle was the subject of it.

He has gradually adapted to his adopted home, more to the women in his life (my wife and daughter) than me. But we are having more good moments than at first. He continues to be terrified of unexpected noises, with motorcycles, school busses, and garbage trucks being the worst. He panics and freezes at anything he is not conditioned to. In the morning I walk him on the path to the east. In the afternoon we walk in the opposite direction to the west. If I try to change the routine and go the wrong way, he will not budge.

One may assume fear will trigger his fight-or-flight response, but you will be wrong. He has no fight response in him. He never even barks. Flight is his only reaction to fear. And that is the introduction to what has caused terror and my life (as I know it) to flash before my eyes. It is all because I have forgotten to grab the ever-present poop bag (for the dog) upon leaving the house.

At the entrance to our walking path, there was a container with poop bags, but it was empty. I noticed there was still a tube inside the container that had a bag left, but I needed to reach inside and try to pull it out, which wasn't easy if one's fingers were not tiny. I tried to reach for a bag, but Bosco wanted to walk and pulled away. I held his leash tight and tried to reach back at the box and succeeded only in making a lot of noise as the lid scraped and the lock rattled. The dog pulled one way, and I pulled the other.

Suddenly, I felt the tension on the leash disappear, just like a long-ago fishing trip when the biggest fish ever hooked got away and the line went slack. In glancing toward Bosco, I noticed him straining to escape the noise. In the process, he slipped out of his harness, which I never imagined possible. Then as if in slow motion, I saw the harness drop to the ground, his collar fly into the air, and Bosco, now free as a bird, in a panic, running away from me and the noisy container I had my hand on. He headed down the path. And this truly all seemed to be in slow motion as I suddenly realized the love of my wife's life, her little Bosco, was heading away from me with a speed that only a beagle in full retreat could muster.

My life, as I knew it, would never be the same. The leash was empty! I couldn't believe it, knowing I was in trouble more than I could imagine. What if I lost him? What if he got hit by a car? Slowly, it dawned on me I had only one choice, and that was to try to chase him down.

You are right to laugh! More slow motion! I quit jogging twelve years and twenty-five pounds ago. I walked four miles or so a day but wasn't certain I could even run a hundred yards, even as my legs started moving and I headed after a little dog that looked to be flying, frightened as he was.

You know the feeling when so much is going on at the same time, and so much information is being processed. I was upset at myself for not noticing his fear as he started pulling away. I was embarrassed someone might see me moving more quickly than normal. I was terrified how I would tell Roxanne I had lost Bosco. And all the while, I was moving (also in slow motion) and just hoped it was not the sunset I was heading into.

I called his name three times, and suddenly, he stopped. He turned around and sat down and looked at me with terrified beagle eyes. I am not sure if the terror was from the noise that caused him to bolt or the sight of me lumbering after him and shouting his name. But he stopped. I got to him, put his leash back on, rubbed his ears, scratched his neck, and told him what a good boy he was. (Sometimes it is best not to be brutally honest!) Then I said a prayer of thanks that I was able to return home safe, sound, and with Bosco back in the fold.

There are times in our lives when prayers of thanksgiving are automatic and truly meaningful. This is one. And in such times, I am always reminded how easily and quickly things can take such a drastic turn that brings only fear and panic. But my next thought is how many times that doesn't happen, and we never give thanks for the ordinary, the expected, and the easy. I will let this remind me to try harder not to take anything for granted and to be thankful more fully and often for all in my life that is more of a blessing and benefit than I take time to remember. This is but another chapter in the saga of a beagle named Bosco and the day when my marriage has survived and I have been able to smile and wonder if beagles have guardian angels. And I am even more convinced that I do!

WINSTON

WE HAVE DEVELOPED SOME SORT of attraction to beagles. Years ago, we rescued one and named him Winston. He smelled, looked, and ate like a beagle. His color was that of a beagle.

We used to joke that our first dog—a white fluffy mixed breed—had an incredible vocabulary. She seemed to know more than single words and even sentences. Winston was somewhat slow in that area and had crooked teeth. He did not have an intelligent demeanor. He was a playful dog but had some qualities that held him back. But we loved him as much as any dog we had.

One evening I took him for his late walk. A guy came walking by and told me that he thought my dog was quite old. I was a little put off by that comment from someone who had never seen and didn't know. It seemed such a weird greeting, and the hair on the back of my neck stood up. I asserted quite forcefully that Winston was only ten. Then the man replied by saying, "I don't think he is really a real beagle. He looks like he has some hound in him."

I thought a beagle was a hound but didn't want to get into an extended conversation with a walking path expert. Worried about references to his family, I stuck up for Winston. I replied that we knew that he was all beagle. But I was a little taken aback by the assault on Winston's pedigree and decided to add more. I shared that what was most important was that he thought he was a beagle and acted like a beagle and that there was no doubt in any of our minds that he was a beagle.

My attempt was to keep my tone friendly, and then we just walked on. That might seem like enough justification to pay for a DNA test, just to be sure, but what would be the purpose? Winston was who he was, and even when he acted out of character, we knew him to be a beagle. This conversation raised an interesting issue for all of us.

Are we confident enough in who we are that comments or questions of others don't throw us off stride? This is such a hypersensitive time in our society that many fear to be labeled as something that they are not. Bullying and character assassination seem somewhat normal these days, and none of us want to be associated with the wrong crowd. I am not sure how we have arrived at such a touchy place, but we are certainly there. Daily, people lose jobs, reputations, appointments, and endorsements simply because their pedigree is in doubt, or they have made judgments on others.

Should a word or action be inappropriate, it certainly needs to be addressed in an appropriate manner that can lead to a positive and helpful response. Sometimes we may also just consider the source and walk away. Unfortunately, we seem to be at a point in our culture where forgiveness and second chances have gone by the wayside. Too many seem to be poised to jump at opportunities to lift themselves by putting other people down. Many fear being stereotyped as someone they are not.

So how secure are you in who you are and what you believe? As loved and forgiven children of God, we have a good start. If we are secure in such faith, we know how we are called to live. If we know whose we are, then we know who we are. Hound? No way. Winston is a beagle. What about you?

MERLE AND HENRIETTA

MERLE AND HENRIETTA WERE MEMBERS of my first congregation. They were in their nineties and extremely frail and had no family or friends. Their house was small, old, musty, and very dark inside. They had lived in this house for seventy years. Merle was a skinny, quiet guy, and Henrietta was his opposite in every way. They were unable to leave their house except for occasional trip to the doctor or grocery store.

From time to time, I would come to their home to visit and offer them Holy Communion as they no longer could participate in worship with the congregation. Merle was almost deaf and mostly blind. Henrietta could barely walk. Both had serious health issues more than obvious to me, but in time, they would be more so.

Three days before Christmas, Merle called, was very emotional, and said Henrietta had fallen out of bed and couldn't move. She outweighed both of us by fifty pounds or more, and I knew we could not get her into bed. I dialed 911 and headed over to their home, arriving just as the paramedics were putting her into the ambulance to take her to the hospital. They informed me she had suffered a stroke.

I visited her later in the hospital. The nurse asked if they had any family, and I told her that I was not aware of any at all. I gave her my name and phone number and told her she could call me if there was any way I could help. I drove by their house and told Merle what was going on and made plans to give him a ride to the hospital later. She seemed to be doing fairly well, and he did as well.

On Christmas at three in the morning, I received a phone call from the hospital informing me that Henrietta had died. The nurse had tried to call Merle, but with his deafness, he never heard the call. They asked if I would drive to his home and inform him of her death. So about thirty minutes later, I was the angel messenger to tell Merle how alone he was really going to be.

I banged and banged on the door, but he didn't answer. Luckily, it was unlocked, and I went in and woke him up. I told him we needed to talk and that I would wait in the living room for him. I would never forget sitting with Merle as I told him Henrietta had died. He sobbed. He cried. He trembled. And then I had to leave him alone as I returned to my family and a congregation's hymns of Christmas joy.

In hindsight, I realized there was another cry that morning I was too busy to hear. It was a sound often silenced by the hustle and bustle of our busy world but one that was filled with beauty, power, and grace. It was the sound of that most holy night in Bethlehem. The sound of which I speak was a birth cry. But that birth cry was different from any the world had ever heard.

Its soothing tones began centuries earlier, building up momentum until its explosion on a starry night over Bethlehem. This birth cry shattered the darkness of a world in sin. It echoed through mountain and valley, past river and stream, into cities and desert places. This birth cry was announced by an angel to Mary and reshaped through the lungs of a baby in a manger. This birth cry would reach its climax as those same lungs, full grown, would breathe their last and cry out from a cross and echo from an empty tomb. "It is finished!"

When I sat with Merle, I was too overwhelmed by his sobs to remember the greater cry of a baby in a manger on that first Christmas Eve. Later, we would talk about that, and for both myself and Merle, it changed the flavor of his tears and added another sound of hope to his grief. We have all had our own "Merle and Henrietta" memories and moments, and it is for those that God has opened our hearts to the full joy of his love. No matter what season, the birth cry of a Savior changes every moment of our lives!

A YELLOW FLAG

I WISH THAT I COULD remember more of the simple, quiet yet wonderful moments in life. It seems that too many memories are of times of dramatic disappointment or tragedy in which we get stuck like a car with tires spinning in a snowbank. There are so many gifts of clarity and joy that too easily slip away like a morning mist. I wish that those memories were easier to retrieve, but for some reason they often seem to elude me.

Thankfully, one such time has not escaped my memory. It was a random, unexpected request from my daughter Abby when she was about four. It made no sense yet taught me a lesson I would never forget.

The year before, Roxanne and I bought one of those little enclosed carts to pull behind a bicycle so we could ride our bikes in the neighborhood and bring Abby along. You have seen those carts with a top and side curtains so an infant doesn't get wet and is blocked from the wind. Her cart had one of those yellow flags on top of a white fiberglass pole so anyone driving a car in the neighborhood would be sure to see something so low to the ground. And of course, it was attached to my bike.

One afternoon I came home for dinner and started to sit in the kitchen to catch up on the day's news. Abby came running in and said, "Daddy, will you take the flag off my cart and stick it in the ground in the backyard?"

I looked at Roxanne, but she seemed caught off guard by the question as well. My typical first reaction was to say, "No, we need it on the cart."

But Abby's mom had been good, over the years, in helping me be careful about knee-jerk reactions and comments. She had helped me learn to catch my breath, keep my calm, and not say anything right away when

I was caught off guard. We both knew that my tendency was to give immediate and initial responses that were not always as sensitive and helpful as they could be. I remembered my training, at least on that day.

And so after an appropriate pause to gather my thoughts, I asked, "Abby, why do you want that little yellow flag to be in the ground in the backyard?"

Without hesitation she answered, "To remind us of Jesus!" Another moment of silence thankfully followed. She had caught me off guard as I knew the flag would be going where she asked. So what if it made no sense?

I took the yellow flag off the cart and planted it in the middle of the backyard. Abby was laughing. She was one happy little kid who beamed from ear to ear. That evening I caught myself wondering why she would think a yellow flag would remind anyone of Jesus! But she was happy, and that was a good enough reason to let it go and move on to more important issues.

Days later I had completely forgotten about the flag, but when I happened to see it fluttering out in back, the first thing that came to my mind was Jesus! That made no sense, and yet she was right! It worked. Like you, I have learned that more than we often give them credit for, our little ones do know what is going on.

BROWN BAG

AS I APPROACHED MY SENIOR year of college, my good news was I had secured a great summer job that would cover most of my tuition for the year. What I hadn't considered was the realities of installing sheets of fiberglass insulation in refrigerators, ovens, and cafeteria line tables in a factory with no air-conditioning during the hot days of summer in Fort Wayne, Indiana.

It was hot, uncomfortable, monotonous, tedious work. I had to wear a flannel shirt buttoned all the way up to my neck, goggles, and thick work gloves. While we had to be concerned about the particles of fiberglass, the sharp edges of the stainless steel panels that were then fastened over the fiberglass were a source of caution as well. If anyone ever asks, sweat and fiberglass insulation are not good partners!

My supervisor was a fifty-year-old guy named Ed, whose education ended after the eighth grade (or sooner). He first worked on his family farm and then got a job in this factory. He was very difficult to work with as conversations were not easy, and he tended to hover over me all the time, even though my tasks were relatively simple. No matter what I did, it was never right.

We constantly butted heads. I was never certain what was worse, his daily criticism or getting fiberglass inside my shirt sleeves and collar. Both got under my skin. The job paid well, but it was not an enjoyable job. I had no idea why we couldn't find common ground. I got used to daily confrontations as he gave instructions that made no sense. Some tasks that could have been done in five minutes took fifteen if I did it his way. I soon learned his way was the only way if I was going to keep a job I needed.

I couldn't wait until the summer ended and I could leave. I was tired of the job. I was frustrated by constantly being criticized when the work we were doing was so menial and boring. Everything got under my collar—sweat, fiberglass, Ed. I found myself trying not to talk at all and hoping that would keep conversations from becoming confrontational. It was just a frustrating time for both of us.

I don't know if my questions weren't understood or were seen as a challenge. Whatever the case, it was obvious he resented my questions and comments. I was frustrated that he talked to me like I was a clueless teenager. That fall and winter, I had worked with two engineers in the factory office, filing drawings and making parts lists. I felt they had treated me as I deserved to be treated. This factory scene was a pain.

Finally, it dawned on me (I am a slow learner) that my only option was to go along with what he said, if for no other reason than respect for his authority. It was a frustrating time. I came to realize we could never be friends but didn't understand why he was so hard to get along with. He probably felt even more so about me. He was one of the few people for whom I found no way to establish common ground even for casual conversation. But my last day of work at the end of summer offered a surprise.

As I was leaving for the last time at the end of our shift, he handed me a brown lunch bag with three tomatoes from his garden. He told me he wanted to thank me for helping him over the summer. This was his gift! I was the one then with little to say. I had judged him and thought he had no ounce of compassion or understanding. He caught me by surprise by his simple act of generosity, which I knew was a big deal for him and something he had thought about for quite a while. He was more complex and caring than I assumed, and it was a wonderful lesson for me to learn. The best gifts are such unexpected surprises!

FIRED

MY FIRST JOB WAS WHEN I was a junior in high school. I worked in a convenience store and often had to close up at eleven in the evening all on my own. From then on, I had various jobs all the way through the seminary. I worked construction, in a bank, in a school cafeteria, and as a short-order cook. I always did the best I could and was given good reviews. During our third year of seminary, we interned at a congregation under the supervision of a pastor. I was assigned to a small congregation in Miami, Florida. Two months into my internship, my supervising pastor left, and the district president asked me to serve as pastor for the rest of the year. Then I returned for my final year at the seminary.

During my first two years at the seminary, all of us were assigned to a local congregation for fieldwork. It was a chance every weekend to gain practical experience in leading worship, teaching, and seeing how a congregation really operated, all under the supervision of the pastor of that church. That was a wonderful two years for me. It was wonderful training in the real world, under supervision, which had saved many congregations from newly minted pastors who had no practical experience.

Those two years were enjoyable and helpful and brought great memories. In my last year at the seminary, I had no such obligation. It was a good thing as I had just gotten married and was working almost full-time as a bank teller to pay for my tuition. One day a pastor of a congregation I had never been to called. He said I had a great reputation from my fieldwork church and asked if he could hire me to help with his youth group.

After a discussion about this with my bride, I agreed to take the weekend job. A little extra money for newlyweds seemed like it was worth the extra work. To make a long story short, I went to that church and never met the pastor, and the counselors and kids really weren't very friendly. I had been given no clarity about what had been going on or what was expected.

A week later, the pastor called to tell me I wasn't fitting in and was fired. I hadn't even have a chance to find out what my responsibilities were! My ego was crushed. My fieldwork church had loved me. My vicarage in Miami was a great success. I had been working since my junior year of high school and had never been fired, until then! All I could think of was how unfair this had been.

As always with hindsight, this did teach me some valuable lessons. I had allowed my ego to cause me to jump into a role without checking it our first. Even being fired was a good experience as it wasn't the end of the world or the worst thing that would ever happen. Remembering such disappointments over the years had taught me to ask more questions before answering and to pay attention to details that might easily be overlooked.

Life is like that for all of us. Life is not about what is fair or unfair but how we live with whatever we face. History doesn't always repeat, and what has worked well once may not again. Just because some people see you in a certain light doesn't mean others will as well (and vice versa). If we expect life to always be fair, we set ourselves up for great disappointment. Sometimes there is nothing to do but shake the dust off our sandals and move on. Even disappointments and failures can become blessings if we find ways to learn from them and allow them to remain in the past, where they belong.

God has certainly helped me figure some things out in this frustration that I never would have learned without it. Blessings certainly do come in all sorts of packages, shapes, and sizes and even when we least expect them!

BIRD ATTACK

I HAVE DONE EVERYTHING I can to make our backyard hospitable for our wildlife. We have flower beds, birdbaths, feeders, and a compost pile, which is a favorite of some of the night-time rodents looking for scraps. I am a friend to wildlife. With that in mind, there is a day when that confident feeling has been suddenly challenged.

Working in our flower bed, I was startled by a robin that buzzed my head. Beyond the surprise, I was confused. I wasn't close to any bird's nests, and I knew that robins don't build nests in flower gardens. It didn't make sense. I was no threat to that bird. I had been minding my business. So what was up? I must have been mistaken, or maybe I overreacted. I turned back to my work. Then I saw the robin coming at me again at full speed, but this time I could see what was really going on.

The first time I was buzzed, I only caught a glimpse as the bird flew by. This time I realized there was not one bird but two in some sort of aerial combat! They both flew by me again, closer than the time before. I ducked, and as I watched them pass by, I realized the robin I thought was coming at me wasn't. It was chasing a cowbird! It had been the cowbird coming my way with a robin in hot pursuit.

It was like a scene from a war movie, and I was ready to hit the dirt if they came at me again. I kept looking around, waiting for the next flyby, but they were both gone. It was the robin that took the blame the first time, but now I realized the culprit had not even been seen until I witnessed the full reality of the situation in their second flyby.

I blamed the robin as that was the only bird I saw, but I realized the cowbird was the culprit, and I was simply an innocent bystander who got in their way. I had blamed the wrong bird. The more I thought about it, the more it made perfect sense.

You see, there is something unique about cowbirds as they have a sneaky habit of not building nests. Instead, they find nests that other birds have built. They wait until those nests have eggs and then lay one or two of their eggs alongside the others. They disappear and never visit those nests or eggs again. Whatever sort of evolutionary process has led to this is beyond me, but apparently they are quite willing to let other birds build nests and raise their hatchlings. This was obviously one time when a cowbird got caught in the act, and the robin was not happy.

Weird, huh? The robin was defending its nest, not attacking me. I just happened to get in the way. How often had I felt I was the object of an attack that was out of the blue and undeserved? And how often had I been tempted to respond with anger or even considered revenge? And yet upon reflection, I often discovered that it really wasn't about me at all but the frustration, grief, or defensiveness of someone else who was lashing out, and I was simply and conveniently in the way.

The robin has been acting on instinct just as we all do. Before overreacting, we often do better to take a deep breath and figure out what is really behind the pain or fear causing another to lash out. And then we can get out of the way or know how we may help.

PARAKEETS IN GERMANY

WE LIVED FOR THREE YEARS in Germany while Dad was assigned to his post in Giessen. I had so many memories of all Mom and Dad did over those years to keep life as normal as they could, but a memorable one was our parakeets in a cage. They were typical pet store parakeets, some green and some blue.

I don't know if they were for Mom or my sisters. I couldn't remember having much to do with them except that sometimes my younger sisters would open the cage, and the parakeets flew around the room, leaving more than a few deposits on the curtains. Then my brother and I were assigned the task of catching parakeets without damaging their little wings. I don't think we had parakeets in the house for very long. Some experiments are doomed from the start.

Many years later, my wife and I were blessed to be able to enjoy a river cruise up the Rhine River, visiting many sights that I remembered from my years there as a child. We made some friends with another couple who sat with us for meals. One night at dinner, the husband showed us several pictures he had taken that afternoon alongside the river in Cologne. It was of a tree that was filled with a flock of parakeets!

Parakeets in Germany? That didn't make sense! I had never heard of wild parakeets in Germany. They are tropical birds, so there is no way this should be!

After a quick Google search, I found several newspaper accounts of small populations of parakeets in several major cities of Germany. The stories weren't very clear about whether they had been blown off course during migration or established populations from birds that were set free by owners who no longer wanted them (you know, just like alligators in the sewers of New York). Whatever the case, there were several small populations along the Rhine, and it seemed they had been able to survive the winters.

Thinking about my incredulity upon hearing of parakeets in Germany, I wondered what the shopkeepers of Bethlehem thought when shepherds said they had seen angels! Or what did Babylonian stargazers think when they followed the star of a king and found a baby in a manger?

Who would have ever expected God to fill the flesh of a baby? And even if God did come to the earth, who would expect it to happen in a manger in a backwoods village called Bethlehem? That surely took the cake, right? Some still claimed it could not happen as it defied the rules of science and logic of common sense. It had to be as weird for people at that time as seeing a flock of wild parakeets in a tree in Germany.

Now I don't know why those parakeets made me think about angels and Bethlehem, but they did. (It must have been the wings!)

But guess what? A baby in a manger changed the world with his life, death, and resurrection, revealing the power and extent of God's love for everyone on this confused and dysfunctional planet. We are fortunate Mary, the shepherds, Matthew, and Luke remembered to tell the story and that Mark, Luke, and Saint Paul added more to the eyewitness accounts to make certain we would know that the unbelievable is true.

Parakeets in Germany? A Messiah in a manger? God's love is so great he has come to us? Grace doesn't always make sense, but what a good deal God shares it anyway. If that isn't a reason to have a special celebration, what is?

PROPHETS

IN A SEMINARY CLASS INTRODUCING us to the Old Testament prophets, our professor began by asking if anyone had seen anything out of the ordinary that morning. It was not a question any of us saw coming. It was an eight o'clock class. Most of us had only been awake a half hour or so. This was not a favorite hour for twenty-two-year-old guys to have to think. As a result, there was nothing but silence.

This professor had a reputation of being incredibly creative and a little different. He sort of resembled what Isaiah or Amos might have looked, with messed-up white hair and rumpled trousers. Maybe it was a trick question. Maybe he had given that as an assignment and I had forgotten. What were we supposed to see? I was clueless and tried to slink down lower so he wouldn't look my way. The room remained silent, and he allowed the silence to grow.

Finally, one brave soul finally spoke up. He said while he was running to class, he noticed a white mushroom as big as a dinner plate! (This caught our attention as we wondered if he had or was simply saying the first thing that came to mind.) Our professor smiled and started asking questions about the mushroom. We started to pay attention and wondered why none of us had seen that mushroom and why it was such a big deal. Gradually we understood our professor's intent.

A prophet proclaims what God has inspired. One can never share a message from God unless he or she first is open to God's efforts to break through our haze.

Old Testament prophets weren't holier or smarter than the average people of Judaea; they were simply those who were watching and listening for God to break through. They were people who, even at eight in the morning, were open to seeing and hearing what they had never seen and heard before. One would never know how God might break into our consciousness today, just as they didn't then. The message of our professor was that people would hear and see God's guidance only by being quiet, observant, expectant, and open to what God might be up to.

The question that morning had nothing to do with mushrooms but everything to do with faithful waiting. Every prophet was called out of the blue. They had not planned to be prophets but somehow were open to God's call.

This is important for us to remember as we are surrounded by voices demanding to be heard or insisting they alone have the answers. If we are too busy listening to the world and making sure others hear us or preoccupied with emotional responses or frustrations, how will we ever sense the presence of God in our midst? If we are asleep at the switch or distracted by nonsense, there is much that we may miss.

It is in silence that we hear and through patient observation that we see. Until we hear God's voice (which is often drowned out by an angry or fearful world), we can too easily be pushed and pulled by the tides of brokenness and fear. A prophet is one who shares what God has shared, and there is nothing worth sharing until God's voice is recognized and embraced. Faithful living is not about knowing all the answers but in recognizing God's voice and seeing the path he creates.

How can anyone hear or see what God shares unless there is a willingness to stop, look, and listen—just in case? It is not our words and wisdom but God's powerful word the world needs now more than ever. Learn from the prophets to allow silence and faithful living.

WELCOME ABOARD

AIRPORTS ARE A DEFINITION OF something that is both a blessing and curse. Flying is supposed to be convenient. It is the first stage to getting us from here to there quickly and comfortably—except that is usually not the case.

Airports involve more waiting than anything else. And when you have to wait, you start looking around as there is little more one can do.

After a long wait at Reagan National Airport for a relatively short flight back to Michigan, I was tired of waiting. Finally, our flight was announced, and everyone rushed to get in line to board the plane. The gate attendant asked for everyone to move back and allow those who needed assistance to board first.

Then she asked if there were military personnel waiting for the flight. Washington, of course, is full of military installations, so it was no surprise that before the rest of us boarded, military personnel were allowed to board first. At least twenty or thirty young men and women walked past the gate to enter the plane. All were in civilian clothing and moved quickly through the gate.

However, the last young soldier was stopped as his boarding pass wasn't readable on the scanner. As the airline attendant was seeking to board the plane quickly, she asked him to wait behind her for a moment until she could get things figured out. He was well over six feet tall and she about a foot shorter, so he towered over her and looked like her bodyguard.

We started boarding, and all had to walk by this young man, who shouldn't have had to wait but made the most of his wait. He smiled as I walked by, and I heard him say to the man just behind me, "Welcome to our Delta flight to Detroit. I hope you have a pleasant and safe journey." As I moved farther down the ramp, I heard him repeat the same phrase again and again. Apparently, he decided to enjoy his time waiting. I looked back at the man behind me, whose smile was as big as mine. We agreed this young man's mother had raised him well.

Random moments such as this not only make life interesting but also reveal much about those around us. He could have been embarrassed or frustrated by having to wait, and yet he chose a different path, making the most of his wait and making the entry onto the plane much more pleasant than usual for a variety of passengers.

How do any of us respond when we are momentarily delayed, slowed down, or pulled out of a normal routine? My guess is his choice of reaction was more positive than many of us had undertaken. He turned that moment into something much more than a typical boarding of an airplane. He made the process more pleasant for those who passed by, and everyone entering the cabin of a jet with a smile was something to behold. Travel by air is not easy with delays, cramped seating, and overbooked planes. But for a moment there were smiles and relaxation for many who had not anticipated anything other than a crowded path down the runway to a crowded plane.

The fact that I was even remembering this moment and having a smile return on an otherwise busy morning for me testified to the impact one could have on many. For him to do so in such a casual, genuine, and creative way was amazing. For some reason, I must have been distracted when he finally entered the cabin as I never saw him again. I wish I could have thanked him. Maybe he didn't even get on the flight. But he had been there. We heard him, and we smiled. What a reminder of how we could affect one another when we put aside our preoccupations and distractions and simply found a way to enjoy the moment, no matter where or what it might be.

NOISES IN THE DARK

ON FAMILY VACATIONS WE EITHER stayed with relatives or camped. It was a matter of economics. We had a Ted Williams camper, which was a small trailer with a foldout tent. Imagine a family of five children under the age of twelve in a station wagon with no air-conditioning. We were on a cross-country trip to Yellowstone, pulling a little camper trailer behind the car.

We had gotten as far as we could on the first leg of our trip. Mom found a campground in our *Rand McNally Road Atlas* in the middle of nowhere, South Dakota. It was an empty field with one outhouse and no other campers! But we needed to stop as the nearest alternative campground was at least twenty miles away, and it would soon be dark.

The tent needed to be set up, sleeping bags to be pulled open, and the Coleman stove to start cooking a meal for seven tired and hungry people. We looked around and decided it wasn't much of a campground. There were no buildings except for a little wooden outhouse on the other side of the field. There was a box to put a payment in for our campsite, and that was it.

It went rather smoothly, until about an hour after the lantern was turned off. There was a noise that didn't sound like one of us. It was a distant but loud cry of some animal. I wondered if anyone else heard it or if they were all as scared as me. For hours that cry continued as some sort of animal wandered around the outside of the field in which we were camped. None of us said a word. And I am sure none of us slept!

All night long the animal kept its cry going. I had never been so scared and expected a wild beast would tear into our tent. Every time I almost fell asleep, that howling in the darkness resumed. We never knew what it was until years later when I heard the same cry from a large cat in the Saint Louis Zoo. It had been a bobcat! Most likely we were safe at the time, but there was no way to know it then.

We all have had similar moments in our lives. No matter how much we try to calm down or be rational, there are situations in which we will are scared, afraid, or worried. It is easy for someone, at such a moment, to tell us to just pray and turn it over to God, which is what we should do, but it isn't always as easy as that, is it? Sometimes the darkness and the unknown can rattle us to the core.

But the reason for a baby in a manger in Bethlehem is to bring assurance we are never alone, no matter how scary the dark may be. When you remember which kitchen drawer holds the flashlight, a power outage isn't quite as disturbing, is it? In the same way, remembering the light Jesus's birth has brought into our darkness can change any of our forays into the shadows.

Long ago, wise men followed that same light and basked in the glow of the surprise of their lives. And we always do as well. It may not always come as quickly as we want, but the proximity to the light Jesus brings will change any of those scary and fearful times of life. The cry of a baby in Bethlehem we cannot see is more comforting than the darkness in our sight. It is always a matter of deciding which noises that surround us will we cling to. My vote goes to the baby in a manger!

SANTA, GO AWAY!

WHAT ARE YOUR TRADITIONS ON Christmas Eve as you get everything ready for the celebration to begin? In our family, Santa, for some reason, never shows up until early on Christmas Day, so there is always time late on Christmas Eve for last-minute preparations. One such time has brought quite a surprise.

There are so many powerful moments in our lives, such as these, that quickly fade away as we get busy and preoccupied with other stuff. Such matters may not be more important, but for a while we assume they are, and soon what is really meaningful is forgotten and disappears like a cloud that floats out of our sight over the horizon.

As we remember to slow down and think of what we have forgotten, we sometimes regain a sense of what is more meaningful and memorable than the windmills we are fighting or the shadows we are chasing. From experience I can speak, as I have been reminded by my wife of a forgotten memory that I don't want to miss ever again.

Like many parents, on Christmas Eve Roxanne or I put out a plate with a cookie and a glass with milk (or maybe scotch) for Santa. My parents had a similar routine so that we would have visual proof that Santa had really been in our house, as evidenced by an empty glass and cookie crumbs. It also gave us a sense of rewarding Santa for his hard work, which every kid wanted to make sure to take advantage of.

When Abby was three, I came home after the midnight worship service to find everyone sound asleep. Roxanne had taken care of the last-minute preparations. As always, Santa's refreshments were on the table nearest the tree. Of course, there was also the obligatory thank-you note to Santa, which I didn't take time to read. In failing to read the note, I missed a surprise that was waiting for him.

The next morning as I was puttering around, I caught sight of the note and, for some reason, decided maybe I should read it. I knew it wasn't the note I had seen earlier in the evening as it was on a different paper and written by a different hand. But I had been too tired when I got home late on Christmas Eve to take a look.

Apparently, Abby had insisted on a special request to her mom and dictated this message she insisted should be left for Santa. Here was the text in all its glory: "Dear Santa, Go away! I am afraid of you. Leave my gifts at my cousins' house. Abby."

She was at that stage where she was struggling with concerns about things that went bump in the night and afraid of what she didn't understand. Roxanne recently reminded me of that forgotten moment, which had brought a smile again. Not only did we remember this moment for its amusement value but it also reminded me how often, in more adult ways, we'd reject what we didn't understand or cause us fear.

There are so many things we wish would just go away or we would never have to face. We find all sorts of ways to avoid and forget, and yet life is full of them. Abby was blunt as only a three-year-old can be, while as adults we tend to hide, pretend, and bury what causes us to be afraid. It is out of love for us that God comes to deal with what we wish would just go away but can't make it happen on our own.

Every year we move from the mountaintop and bright lights of Christmas to the darker valley of Lent. It is our reminder that Jesus has come to take on the dark shadows and scary moments of life so we learn we are not alone and no longer need to hide from what we fear. And the proof of his power and love is not an empty plate or cup but an empty cross and tomb so things that go bump in the night and cause even mature adults to tremble are held at bay. This is also a wonderful reminder that God reads our notes to him before we even write them or know what to say.

GUILT GONE

HOW DO YOU HANDLE MOMENTS and feelings of guilt, especially one that just can't seem to go away or too late to do anything about? There are so many ways that we hurt or ignore others and so many situations we wish we could revisit and change. But the past is always history, and guilt is one of the most difficult issues for any to deal with.

We wish we could change what we cannot, and we have trouble finding peace as we reflect on missed opportunities or mistakes that haunt us. Guilt is a powerful force that can hold us back like a lead weight or an anchor dragging behind us. Our embarrassment due to guilt is a force with greater influence on tomorrow than we understand or admit. So until whatever guilt or shame we carry is buried or removed, no amount of resolve will allow us the freedom to become what we are capable of being.

For years I was troubled by something I had done as a six-year-old. It was so selfish and disrespectful to my dad that I never could get that image out of my mind. It hadn't even been malicious but simply something a six-year-old was prone to do without thinking. It was not the only thing I wish I could have changed in my behavior as a child or even as an adult. But for some reason, this one moment continued to haunt me years later.

It was not until I was able to talk to Dad many years later that I could resolve that guilt. One summer I was with him and Mom, and he and I were all alone. I reminded him about that day, what I did, and how it still troubled me. He said nothing at first. His response was he couldn't even remember it had happened.

I realized that decades earlier, maybe even that same day, he had let go of what I was hanging on to for too long. In that exchange, I understood better than I ever had before the power of forgiveness and grace. My father's actions defined grace. And I understood as well that I could not erase guilt for my actions because they stood the test of time. Someone else had to free me from my imprisonment.

As Christians we easily use words like *grace* to describe God's love but fail to put them into practice in our own living. The result is that guilt often is allowed free rein and has more power over us than we are aware. Guilt is nothing more than allowing the past to control our present.

If we only believe what we say we believe, we will discover how much easier it is to break free from the anchor of guilt than we have ever imagined. There is so much we cannot change, but God's love allows us to walk away from a guilty past to freely do what we could have done in the first place. Forgiveness allows us a fresh beginning every day! Rather than be burdened by what we cannot change, we are called to joyfully and lovingly do now what we really can and should do. With guilt off the table, all sorts of possible new scenarios exist.

Take Christ's gift of forgiveness to heart. Rather than beat ourselves over and over again for what cannot be changed, why not use the passion of our new lives to become the light in the darkness God has always had in mind for us to be?

It seems too easy to simply accept forgiveness without having to pay burdensome fines, which is what grace is all about. This is a love we do not deserve, but having been blessed with such an incredible gift, how can we not live with a commitment to a new today and tomorrow that is free from the weight restrictions and burdens that guilt seeks to impose?

Grace alone sets us free. Believe it, accept it, and allow freedom rather than the burdens of guilt to be the power and energy of today and tomorrow. If you make any resolutions about tomorrow, let them begin with the freedom of grace, which wipes every slate clean!

BEST CHRISTMAS PAGEANT EVER

EVERY YEAR ZION'S CHILDREN WOULD help prepare us to welcome a baby in a manger with songs, costumes, and readings. They had always done a great job, but one year they literally rocked my house as they played their parts well, and none of the little ones wandered off or escaped. The children opened up our time of worship, which meant I had to follow them!

What an impossible task for an old guy when children are the warm-up act! Thankfully, worship is not about competing but about finding as many ways as possible to nourish and celebrate faith. It is humbling to follow youngsters dressed as angels, sheep, shepherds, and wise men, but I assure you it is inspiring as they have helped me remember what true joy really is!

This particular year I sat in the front row, and it was even more interesting than I imagined it might be. I was closest to sweet little angels adorned with tinsel halos, white angel outfits, and butterfly wings almost as big as the girls themselves. At different moments in their program, each started adjusting and flexing their wings as if suddenly remembering there was something behind them. Was the way wings were attached uncomfortable, or were they afraid their wings would fall off? I couldn't tell. But one by one, I noticed each turn, trying to look behind to see what their wings were up to. They were like novice angels who had just been granted wings and were trying to figure out what they were for or how to make them work. That became my amusement as I tried to guess what was going on in the minds of these part-time angels and their preoccupation with silver-tipped wings.

Then I was pulled back into reality as I noticed movement in front of the stage, and a three-year-old sheep was beginning to gradually wander from her spot, appearing ready for an escape. Now we were getting to the good stuff that every pageant was remembered for, when a little one wandered beyond the control of adults! A sheep is fully grown at three years, but a three-year-old human is a different animal. Then the unexpected happened. A five-year-old wise man saw the impending disaster unfolding and slowly moved toward the wandering sheep, held both of his arms out to the side, and gently shepherded her back to her spot on the stage.

Now we were in business. The story within the story was unfolding. Was he cast wrongly as a wise man when he should have been a shepherd? Or was his ability to multitask and do whatever was required a sign of his wisdom and proper casting? You see, this was the weird stuff that went on in my mind when someone else got to share the message, and I was able to sit back and watch, wonder, and be amazed by the inspiration little children were capable of sharing without even a second thought.

One of the readers was a donkey, I think, and his costume was as creative as that of the angels. So we had a talking donkey reading part of the Christmas story. How cool was that? I mean, we had read storybooks to our children where one of the animals had something to say about being near the baby Jesus, but I couldn't remember a Christmas program with a talking donkey. Or maybe my aging brain cells caused me to imagine or create my own version of what was going on. But it was a magical moment with shades of the movie *Shrek*. And the donkey (at least I think he was a donkey) read very well. I loved it!

The program continued with another attempt at escape, and a different character (hidden from me by the angels) was able to corral the distracted and wandering sheep. That was when I noticed the sheep was holding a cell phone! I couldn't remember that in Luke's account of Christmas, but somehow it didn't seem to be out of place at all. Later, I found out the phone was a clever prop from Mom and Dad to keep her focus on something other than escaping.

So it was a typical children's program, which was enjoyed by all. My front row seat gave me insights others might have not been privy to, but it also reminded me how powerful this story was for children.

I wonder why so many adults have lost that joy and excitement about this most holy night. Too many complain or grumble, worry or fear, or simply don't have time with busy schedules to remember and bask in the pure joy of this good news. The kids have reminded us again that this is the story that should color all our life stories.

While adults obsess with fears of weather, wars, job insecurity, or health concerns, little children are so fascinated by a baby in a manger that they can't wait to be part of the story. That is what I have witnessed yesterday with a talking donkey, brand-new angels learning to flex their wings, and a sheep (or a lamb or something with fur) trying to escape while a wise man gently nudges her back on track. When we learn to see Christmas through the eyes of a child, we are brought out of our adult clumsiness and remember what pure and innocent joy this birth is all about. When we allow children to lead us, we remember that often what we make so important is not significant at all. And this is a story that invites us always to be part of!

Even a wise man whose felt crown is so big it almost covers his eyes has brought me back to the simple joy and love this miracle is all about. The kids get it! And they have again helped us get it too. It is simply about the joy of a baby in a manger and a story too good to leave forgotten or untold!

MARY'S LOST HAND

A UNIQUE EARTHLY TREASURE OF Zion is the hand-carved, painted wooden Nativity set from Oberammergau, Germany. To give a sense of scale, the adult figures are several feet high. Everyone enjoys this manger scene, which consists of Mary, Joseph, a manger, wise men, shepherds, cows, and sheep. It is a complete cast of characters, displayed within a wooden stable and a straw-covered floor. Unique to this set are young children.

While the adult figures stand and gaze, the children are in motion, running to the manger. The expressions of the adults are solemn, while those of the children are full of wonder and joy. And there are as many children as adults! Mary, Joseph, and wise men are dressed as we see in every Christmas pageant.

One year we decided to wait until Christmas Eve to put baby Jesus in the manger. As any change among Lutherans would do, it prompted much discussion. Gradually, the rationale became apparent as little children would ask, "Where is baby Jesus?" And parents were gifted with a shared moment of teaching about that holy night. Rather than just a manger scene, it had become a teaching tool moving us from Advent waiting to Christmas joy.

Recently, I learned another fact that added a new twist. It was about the year Mary's hand was lost! As I said, these were wood-carved figures, obviously more fragile than mass-produced synthetic characters. One year when the set was taken down and put into storage, someone discovered one of Mary's hands was lost. It had been broken off! No one confessed to the accident, and no one knew where to look for Mary's hand. Trying to find a replacement for Mary would take time, and a new carved figure would be incredibly expensive and impossible to perfectly match the rest of the set.

One couple at church was acquainted with a German wood-carver in Frankenmuth. They decided to see what suggestions he might have. The woman who shared this story told me she and her husband wrapped Mary in a blanket and drove her to Frankenmuth to see what the wood-carver would suggest. (That image alone stirred up many thoughts!)

The wood-carver said he was sure he could carve and paint a replacement hand, but it would take time. As it was almost a year before Christmas, he was certain he could have a new hand for Mary in time for the next Christmas season. And he did! Mary's lost hand wasn't found, but it was replaced, and I am not sure, until now, how many people even suspected what had happened. And this couple was even more moved when the elderly German wood-carver refused any payment for his work.

Years ago there was a famous radio personality who shared stories in which he included facts most had never known before. He ended each of his broadcasts with "And now you know the rest of the story." This is a little different as we already know the rest of this story. But there are some twists and turns added today that introduce some color to a familiar scene at Zion.

We live in a world of replacements, and many are not even aware of an earlier time when broken items have been taken somewhere to be fixed or repaired. Today most of what is broken is sold for scrap, given to Goodwill, recycled, and replaced with something new. Think about it. Mary's hand has been lost, and now she is as good as new. In the same way, we have been lost and now are found. Christmas is about broken lives and the healing the miracle of the manger brings.

Christmas is, after all, about taking what has been lost and restoring it to be good as new. That is why the miracle of a baby in a manger is so important that the entire world stops to take notice. As I think about wrapping Mary in a blanket and driving her to a far-off location to be restored, it makes me think of an even longer journey that it has taken for a baby to come from heaven to earth so that the broken and lost parts of our living may be repaired, healed, and made whole.

No one knows what that first Christmas Eve looked like, how people were dressed, or how many shepherds and animals were wandering around. But this manger scene is a visual way of depicting what is difficult to imagine. And just as waiting for baby Jesus to show up in the manger when we don't really want to wait, so knowing about Mary's hand being repaired is a wonderful reminder of what this miracle is truly about and how it has changed you and me.

AIRPLANE WEDDING

AS A YOUNG, INEXPERIENCED PASTOR, I was afraid to ever say no. Whether it was due to my lack of confidence or possibly Lutheran guilt, I never said no to requests. I didn't want to disappoint anyone or seem uncaring. And so rather than take a few moments to digest a request, I typically too quickly just agreed. One day that tendency led me to encounter a situation my seminary classes had never covered.

A neighboring pastor with a large congregation was the darling of the city. He had a successful radio and television ministry. He was larger than life, until one day he suddenly and unexpectedly died. Such moments always rocked everyone's boat. But after a few weeks, people like me who were not immediate family or close friends resumed life as normal. Or so I thought.

One morning the phone rang in my office, and the secretary from that pastor's congregation was on the phone. She was going through his schedule and realized he had promised a couple in his congregation that he would do a private wedding ceremony for them. He had not told his secretary, and the wedding was supposed to be the next day. She was in a panic, and since we were the next closest congregation, she asked if I would be willing to do the marriage.

Without hesitation I assured her I would. I felt pretty important being the one she called to do the wedding for this beloved pastor. It was an honor to be chosen. Of course, I would help out! But there was another detail she had not gotten to yet. The couple both were pilots and had planned to be married in a small Cessna airplane. The secretary conveniently neglected that minor detail until after I had agreed. The wedding was to be the next day at noon.

I had never been in a small plane and am not particularly fond of heights. Immediately, I started considering all the things that could go wrong and wished I had asked more questions before my pride got in the way of prudence. I called the couple and got the details from them about the fact there were only four seats in the plane. The fourth person, who I assumed was the pilot, would be the witness and would also sign the license. I didn't sleep well that night and the next day met them at the airport. Their friend and I were both told to get in the plane first, and I was surprised to see him sit in the back seat next to me rather than where the pilot was to supposed to be.

They both got in, and it became obvious the bride was going to fly the plane, and her husband-to-be would be in the copilot seat. She explained they both loved to fly small planes, and that was why they wanted to get married in a plane. Before I had a chance to change my mind, we were airborne and headed south at about three thousand feet over the farmlands of Northwest Ohio.

I almost forgot why we were in the plane and was trying to remember their names. I never realized how noisy a small plane was. It was warm, and I felt trapped. It was a beautiful day, and seeing all the farms, ponds, and country roads from only a few thousand feet up was pretty interesting, but I was in a plane with people I didn't know, and the bride was the pilot. We were flying south from Toledo, and as we approached Findlay, the bride turned around to face me in the back seat and told me the plane was on autopilot, and now it was time. Time for what?

Then I remembered. I was doing a wedding! I was beyond my initial fears as we seemed to be doing OK, and the weather was calm, but we were all about two feet from one another, and it seemed weird to go through the liturgy of a normal wedding service with all the prayers, readings, and message as preparation for the vows and rings. All I could think about was getting back on the ground.

In my nervousness, I told them I was ready to start, but they had to promise they would not be consummating the wedding until after we landed. Why that came out I'd never know, especially with people I had never met. But nervous humor seemed to help me, and they laughed, and everything, for me, suddenly calmed down. I quickly had them repeat vows, said a quick blessing, and told them they were now married, and it would be OK to head back to the airport and land.

In hindsight, it was no big deal, but at the time I was overwhelmed. I imagine my seminary professors would have enjoyed critiquing my nervous performance but also knew none of my classmates had yet had an experience like that. As long as we landed safely, it would all be OK.

As we approached the runway and were about fifty feet off the ground, an alarm went off, and the engine stopped. Panic! Then the groom said, "Perfect landing!" And we touched down. I asked and was told the alarm was a warning that the plane was about to stall but that it was a good landing, and that had been her goal. Easy for her to say as I kept remembering the alarm going off while we were still off the ground. But it was an interesting moment. And it helped me learn that sometimes it is better to ponder a request or question before responding too quickly. And that had served me well (when I remembered).

BREAKING CHRISTMAS

WHY ARE WE SO EXCITED about Christmas in December, and yet by January (inly in the summer) we wander off back into the desert? If Christmas is such a big deal, why is it only important for such a short time? Should it not be the gift that colors every day? I think we can agree that it should, but no one is perfect, and even in the midst of the wonderful world of Christmas morning, we just can't help ourselves, and the baby in the manger somehow gets lost in the glitz and glitter of a broken world.

My worst Christmas ever was all my fault. And not only was it a disappointment for me but like ripples that spread in a pond, I was not the only one affected as well.

My younger brother was a budding cowboy, and we were both avid fans of Hollywood and television Westerns. All Donny wanted for Christmas was a plastic rifle just like he saw on our favorite show called *The Rifleman*. He made certain his wishes were known, and most likely he wrote more than one letter to Santa that year to make sure his wishes were properly recorded.

His smile on Christmas, as he realized he had gotten exactly what he hoped for, was incredible. It was his best Christmas ever! He was so excited, and I was so jealous.

The day after Christmas, I decided that I should have a turn with his rifle. I asked him to give me a turn, but he wasn't ready to let go. Since he had carried it to bed with him the night before, I should have had a clue that he wasn't about to let go. But my selfishness was more important than the joy on his face as he carried his special gift. I grabbed for his gift.

We wrestled, and I pulled the gun out of his hands and demanded some time with it. In the process the plastic barrel cracked. Less than twenty-four hours from our worship of the Christ child, I had ruined his gift. Christmas was over for him through no fault of his own. The Christ child had somehow been forgotten by me!

We are embarrassed that this is often so true. We are filled with the joy and peace of Christmas as we sing "Joy to the World." But life returns so quickly to normal as if the peace that God has gone to so much trouble to bring to the earth were not enough. Why does it seem impossible for us to keep the Christmas spirit bubbling for more than a few days or weeks? Too often, once the gifts are behind us and daily routines return, we have forgotten why the message of Christmas angels has been enough to get shepherds to leave fields and run through town with such joy in their hearts.

As kids, our selfishness takes on different forms from how we exhibit it as adults, but the result is the same. Gifts are broken, promises are forgotten, and love is withheld. Joy is supplanted by fear, envy, jealousy, and sadness. So easily we forget, and so quickly we go back to fields and flocks as if nothing special had happened. This memory is a good one for me as it reminds me how easily that change can happen. Thankfully, forgiveness can heal real brokenness. And finding time to remember the joy of a baby in a manger is a wonderful way to keep from sliding into old habits. And no matter what month of the year it may be, there is no reason not to be changed by Christ's birth.